Praise for *Tennis for Kids*

"A creative way to get children involved in tennis."
> —ANDRE AGASSI, OLYMPIC GOLD
> MEDALIST, FORMER NUMBER 1 IN MEN'S
> TENNIS

"Kids love to have fun and they enjoy competition. Reggie's competitive games for children of all ages and ability introduces them to the game in such an exciting fun filled way they don't even know they're learning! Learning the fundamentals and having fun at the same time will hopefully 'hook' the kids for a lifetime of tennis!"
> — TOM GULLIKSON, UNITED STATES DAVIS
> CUP CHAMPION, U.S.A. OLYMPIC COACH

"Finally, someone found a way to make practice fun! Reggie's way of tennis has so much variety that kids will . . . keep on with tennis for a long time. This book will help kids . . . love tennis, like I do."
> —MARTINA HINGIS, NUMBER 1 IN WOMEN'S TENNIS

"Tennis coaches understand that to develop talent young players should be exposed to coordination in hand, eye, and movement. The biggest challenge is to make these development exercises fun for young players. In this respect Reggie Vasquez Jr. has done a tremendous job of putting together a very thorough plan of developing tennis skills through fun games. I am sure that his book will be very beneficial to the growth of tennis!"
> — DENNIS VAN DER MEER, PRESIDENT AND FOUNDER
> OF UNITED STATES PROFESSIONAL TENNIS REGISTRY

"As a college tennis coach, who has prepared students both academically and in athletics, for over a decade, it is clear to me that Reggie's book has the potential to spark a love for the game of tennis in a powerful way. His games provide essential early stepping stones for young children to develop skills, in an atmosphere of fun! Reggie's authentic, holistic approach provides a feast for the imagination, an encyclopedia full of ideas—for both coaches and children."
> — DICK GOULD, STANFORD UNIVERSITY
> MEN'S TENNIS HEAD COACH

More Praise for *Tennis for Kids*

"This book is a refreshing new way to teach kids the game of tennis—kids are always more responsive to learning . . . in such a fun way."
— WAYNE FERREIRA,
MEN'S TENNIS PROFESSIONAL

"Reggie's book combines the technical skill of tennis with the movement skills that youngsters need to become better overall athletes. I can't think of a better way to involve children in the sport of tennis and develop their athletic ability at the same time."
— DONALD A. CHU, PH.D., UNITED STATES TENNIS
ASSOCIATION SPORTS SCIENCE COMMITTEE

"Reggie Vasquez Jr. has exposed the game of tennis for what it really is: a blast! One peek at his book and you'll have your kids and students begging to play Tapeworms and Lighthouse. I can't wait until my son is old enough to bug me to drag him—and this book—down to the local courts."
— DAVID HIGDON, SPORTSWRITER,
SENIOR WRITER, *TENNIS MAGAZINE*

"The challenge for tennis is to get kids to try tennis and to stay with it. If it isn't fun they will gravitate to one of the other many optional activities available. Reggie's games will keep them hooked on tennis!"
—CLIFF DRYSDALE, TENNIS COMMENTATOR
ESPN, ABC SPORTS

"Tennis is a wonderful gift for players of all ages, especially children. Reggie Vasquez Jr., has introduced tennis in a creative, fun-filled manner."
— PETER BURWASH, INSTRUCTION EDITOR,
TENNIS MAGAZINE

"Reggie has an outstanding package of material for anyone who loves kids, loves the game of tennis, and loves to have fun! Learning is fun! Now we have the right tool to teach the future of tennis, how to play like champions!"
— LUKE AND MURPHY JENSEN, FRENCH
OPEN DOUBLES CHAMPIONS

Still More Praise for *Tennis for Kids*

"Reggie has written a great book for beginning tennis players. His enthusiasm for the game is obvious when reading his original approach to children's tennis and will not only ignite their love for the game but will enable local coaches to maintain it."

— GRANT CONNELL, FORMER NUMBER 1 IN MEN'S DOUBLES

"If playing tennis were as much fun from the get-go as kicking around a soccer ball or swinging a baseball on a tee, it would probably be the most universally played game in the world. But it is not, and keeping kids interested and focused long enough to master the fundamentals to this complex game is an eternal challenge for coaches. Thanks to Reggie Vasquez Jr.'s innovative and engaging book, that challenge will now be considerably less formidable for parents and coaches smart enough to tap into this neat volume."

—PETER BODO, SENIOR WRITER, *TENNIS MAGAZINE*

"Finally, a book written 100 percent for children! Everyone knows that learning must be fun, but Reggie Vasquez Jr. has showed it in an outstanding way. Not only will kids have fun while learning tennis but they will naturally learn to love the game as well."

—JACK GROPPEL, PH.D. HEAD OF U.S.T.A. SPORTS SCIENCE COMMITTEE, INSTRUCTION EDITOR, *TENNIS MAGAZINE*

"The most fundamental imperative in teaching tennis to children is to make it fun. Reggie has captured this in a wonderful way! I have trained more than 100 world-class athletes, including Jim Courier, Monica Seles, and Aranxta Sanchez Vicario, and Olympic gold medal speed skater, Dan Jansen. All of these athletes' psychological foundations have been formed on the basic concepts of enjoying and loving their sports. The key is right here in this book—fun!"

—DR. JAMES E. LOEHR, SPORTS PSYCHOLOGIST

And Still More Praise for *Tennis for Kids!*

"I believe that Reggie's book of games will revolutionize the way coaches teach young children. Having known Reggie for many years, both as friend and colleague, it's no surprise that he has written a fantastic new book for kid's tennis. His book is sound in both technique and tactics, but more importantly these components are ingeniously hidden behind themes, role playing, and goals in each game. Coaches, parents, and teachers will use this book as 'the' guide to teaching kid's tennis!"

—LOUIS CAYER, CANADIAN DAVIS CUP CAPTAIN, CANADIAN OLYMPIC COACH

"Teaching beginning tennis players is challenging. Reggie's games not only make it fun for the student, but give teaching pros a proven guide from which to work."

—TODD MARTIN, FORMER NUMBER 5 IN MEN'S TENNIS, CURRENT NUMBER 12

"It's great to see tennis being taught to kids in such a competitive way while still maintaining fun!"

—MALIVAI WASHINGTON, FORMER NUMBER 11 IN MEN'S TENNIS

"Hey! These are very original and fun games. I think the hardest thing to do when trying to teach kids a new sport, particularly one that requires so much concentration and skill, is to keep their attention. Reggie seems to have found a way to show kids some new skills, while not forgetting that they need to have fun while they learn. I encourage kids of all ages who are learning how to play tennis to try some of these games. I wish that when I was a kid someone had thought of ways to keep it exciting, because tennis is a very repetitive sport. The only way to get better is to do it over and over and over again. Here is a way to do that but have fun at the same time, and I think it's great. I congratulate Reggie on his vision!"

—GIGI FERNANDEZ, OLYMPIC GOLD MEDALIST, FORMER NUMBER 1 IN WTA TOUR DOUBLES

A Parent's Perspective on *Tennis for Kids*

"I e-mailed you some time ago from South Africa with regards to my son, Jean-Martin (7). At the time I told you I was in the process of ordering your book *Tennis for Kids* via a local bookstore. Well, it arrived and since then I've steadfastly worked my way through your practice drills for kids. Initially, as I paged through the book, I thought many of the exercises sounded almost silly and that my son was far too advanced to waste time on them. *Wow, was I wrong!*

Not having a tennis background myself, I have been reading up on a lot of tennis (even enjoying some player biographies) and now look at your exercises from a whole new perspective. *They are brilliant!* Taking one exercise per category (self-rally; team; projection; reception and rally) per practice session, *Jean-Martin has come to love the game of tennis.* That, in itself, has already made the purchase of your book worthwhile.

But, in addition, his tennis has improved dramatically—not because of tiresome and serious drill exercises—but because he has been developing basic motor skills that coaches normally overlook in favor of more conventional drills.

Recently, during Tennis South Africa Day at Mitchells Park Tennis Club, he played in a mini tournament and was very chuffed when he won the final. A tribute, I dare say, to your input via *Tennis for Kids.* Though I coach my son one-on-one most of the time, some kids at his school asked if they could play, so we've made it a standing arrangement that on *Thursday afternoon everybody gets to participate in Reggie's fun games.* The kids love it, and the other day I had about eight kids come to the court asking if they could play as well.

Well, I thought I'd let you know that under the blistering sun on hardcourts here in South Africa, Reggie's ideas are well and truly represented.

Warm regards,
Johan

TENNIS FOR KIDS

Over 150 Games to Teach Children the Sport of a Lifetime

Reggie Vasquez Jr.

A Citadel Press Book
Published by Carol Publishing Group

To my mom, dad, brother, sisters, and Willow, who have always supported me in my life. Mom and Dad, thanks for your unconditional love, unending generosity, and selflessness.

To all the tennis students that I have taught through the years, especially Laura Ozolins.

And to my friend Stan Smith, a "living legend."

A Citadel Press Book
Published by Carol Publishing Group
Citadel Press is a registered trademark of Carol Communications, Inc.

Editorial, sales and distribution, and rights and permissions inquiries should be addressed to Carol Publishing Group, 120 Enterprise Avenue, Secaucus, N.J. 07094.

In Canada: Canadian Manda Group, One Atlantic Avenue, Suite 105, Toronto, Ontario M6K 3E7

Carol Publishing Group books may be purchased in bulk at special discounts for sales promotion, fund-raising, or educational purposes. Special editions can be created to specifications. For details, contact Special Sales Department, Carol Publishing Group, 120 Enterprise Avenue, Secaucus, N.J. 07094.

Designed by Andrew B. Gardner

ISBN: 0-8065-2123-6

Manufactured in the United States of America

10 9 8 7 6 5 4 3 2 1

This books was originally published by Carol Publishing Group under the title *Kids' Book of Tennis*

Library of Congress Cataloging-in-Publication Data

Cataloging Data for this publication can be obtained from the Library of Congress.

Contents

Foreword

The key for kids to gain interest and maintain enthusiasm for the game of tennis is to make it—fun! The initial positive experiences with the game are vital for a lifelong involvement on the court.

Reggie Vasquez Jr. has developed games that are fun for children to play, while at the same time teaching the basics skills including hand-eye coordination, feel, spin, and ball control. Kids can learn (without knowing it) while having a great time competing, playing, and looking forward to the next time they can get back on the court.

For years pros, including myself, have been trying ways of introducing tennis effectively to young players. Many have made up games for kids to play instead of boring drills to get their points across and to keep the youngsters' interest. So using games is not brand new. But this book is really the first of its kind. It contains over 150 games which are unusual; easy to learn, stimulating, and at the same time incorporate specific goals or tasks for the players. These games will stimulate children's intellectual abilities as well as their creativity and imagination. The games are also adaptable to different levels of players since the difficulty of the tasks can be increased.

Parents and kids have appreciated Reggie's love for the game and his interesting and enthusiastic way of communication with his students. The kids soon identify their favorite games and want to play them time and time again. You don't find that eagerness with the typical drills that most pros use.

I believe this approach of introducing the game is what tennis needs as it competes with other sports and activities for the time and energies of our young people. Once the children get hooked through these games, they may well be hooked on tennis for life—after all, this is the sport of a lifetime!
—Stan Smith U.S.T.A.
Associate Director of Player Development

A Word of Encouragement
From Nick Bollettieri

Nick Bollettieri has coached some of the finest young professionals in the game. He has this to say:

I have been in the business of coaching tennis for nearly forty years. Never in my life have I been more aware of the needs of children than today. I am an American who lives in the most advanced industrialized country in the world. Our neighbors to the north in Canada share the blessings that have been bestowed upon us. For all the freedom, the education, the technological advancements, and the wealth that we possess, we have neglected our children and have allowed our inner cities to deteriorate.

I have believed for quite a while that it would help to create a series of games that produce success and self-esteem in children. And we must accomplish this while the children are in their most formative years. We must help our kids make the connection between hard work and the ultimate success that will surely result, while at the same time not fearing the failures that are also sure to occur. If we can instill these lessons in children before (or as) they learn to play tennis, this sport and all the other challenges that life has to offer will be negotiable. We must teach our children to deal with adversity and enjoy challenge. We must teach our children that a failure to succeed only indicates that an adjustment is required in order to succeed. We must teach our children that thoughtful persistence cannot be defeated.

I believe that Reggie's games will help children to get hooked on tennis. Once that is accomplished, getting hooked on success is simple.

WHAT'S IT ALL ABOUT: TENNIS FUN-da-MENTALs!

The word *fun-da-mentals* implies two things: solid groundwork, a strong foundation. It is critical in the proper development of a young tennis player's game, and, somewhat more creatively, tennis should always be *mentally* fun.

All over the world today, children and adults, some of them handicapped, play tennis. The sport can be enjoyed by anyone who is interested in participating in physical activity. Youngsters as early as three years old can begin "playing tennis" through games and drills that promote fun physical activity and develop motor skills, creating a strong foundation for not only tennis but many other sports.

A simple definition of the game of tennis: A special racquet is used to hit a ball over a net, within a specific boundary, while making it difficult for the opponent(s) to return it. The game of tennis is versatile. It can be played formally: adhering to the traditional scoring system, court boundaries, playing surfaces, rules and regulations, or it can be played casually: for the enjoyment of limited parts of the game, perhaps focusing on certain strokes or tactics. It can be played with friends or even alone, with a wall or a tennis-ball-feeding machine standing in for an opponent.

There are two primary forms of tennis: singles matches and doubles matches. A singles game pits one player on one side of a net against an opponent positioned on the other. Doubles tennis is a team game that can be played with a partner of the same gender or opposite gender ("mixed doubles"). In all tennis matches the goal is to accumulate points to win "games," which in turn lead to "sets," which, when a player wins two of three sets or three of five sets results in victory or "match." Scoring is point by point, called out as follows: "love" (zero), "fifteen" (one point), "thirty" (two points), "forty" (three points), and "game" (winning point). A game must be won by two points, so it often goes on well beyond the first possible "game" point. The finer details of scoring are best dealt with during play.

As children play the games offered in this book, they will surely learn to love the game of tennis—but tennis can be much more than just a game. As Stan Smith declared earlier, it can be the sport of a lifetime.

Following is an overview of my coaching techniques and its goals. Above all, I want young players to enjoy learning the endlessly exciting sport of tennis.

INTENTION

The book can be used as a resource for teaching a variety of games or as a simple teaching methodology for kids. Beneath each fun game façade lie skills development and objectives. Playing these games, younger children will develop various motor skills, older kids will develop basic ball control skills while others will work on mini tennis fundamentals. The games can be used as part of any coach's lesson plan or as a tool to help with lesson plans. By selecting several games from each game category, a lesson plan can be created. The combinations and uses of these games/drills are endless. As you'll soon discover, most children are mesmerized by the themes and role playing of each game. Imagination and role playing are prerequisites when using this book!

This book is not intended to endorse any specific teaching method. Rather its ideas and concepts can be applied to any technique used by coaches interested in teaching young children to play tennis.

WHY USE GAMES?

Some coaches use complex and complicated explanations of tennis when presenting the game to young tennis players. As a result, students may become confused and frustrated and give up trying to learn the game. I believe that it is better to teach tennis basics by using games that are fun to play.

For example, a traditional coach might explain the topic of balance this way:

"Okay, Sammy, let's see if you can be balanced when hitting balls. Your torso should be upright; your feet should make a strong base of support, and your head should be balanced with your chin facing forward. Make sure to keep your center of gravity low and forward."

Most kids don't understand this type of long-winded and boring directions. If instead a coach suggested playing a fun game that would indirectly guide the player to perform an action requiring good balance, imagine how many more children could be attracted to the sport. If good balance on court is indeed the goal, a coach might suggest playing "Bodybuilder," (page 113) in which kids can learn how to control their center of gravity. After a ball is hit each player must immediately pose like a Roman statue or professional bodybuilder. Simple games like this one can quickly bring the desired results.

COMMUNICATION TOOLS

Voice Tone

Based on my own experience and from observing other coaches, I've learned that the tone in which we speak is often more important than the words themselves. There is nothing more boring than a teacher who speaks in a monotone without ever hitting a statement with an exclamation point. Imagine saying to a student "Great job—you did it" in a low monotone; then try saying it with a dramatic change of tone and then ending the statement with an exclamation point in your tone. There is a huge difference! *Rule:* Use a change of tone to emphasize a statement's importance; this will encourage energy and enthusiasm in young players.

Vocal Sounds

Sound is basic to human communication. A baby cries when he or she is hungry or needs to be changed. A subtle, "Aaaahhhhh" or a loud "Wooooo-wooooooo"—sounds that really don't mean anything by themselves—when used in a coaching situation can indicate a coach's praise or excitement. Try using sounds instead of words; ask players to communicate with each other just using sounds or give feedback with sounds more than words. It works! A wordless shout can indicate fear, anger, or delight. Listen to kids playing in a playground, and you'll hear a lot of communication through the use of sounds alone. *Rule:* Use creative sounds to bring home a point.

Have you ever watched a video at home when the phone rang and you had to turn down the volume to take the call? If so, you know that when you look back at the screen, the impact of the video is *much* lower without the sound.

THE BODY AS A LOUDSPEAKER

Facial Expressions

Whenever we speak with another we use not only words but feelings, communicated especially through facial expression. The facial contortions of one of today's hottest actor/comedians, Mr. Jim Carrey, make millions of people around the world laugh. When he says a line in one of his movies, watch his expressions—his face could be rubber; he's incredible. Try this exercise: Have someone speak a sentence with his back to you, then tell him to say it once again facing you and using a strong facial expression, especially with his eyes and eyebrows. *Rule:* Give feedback through facial expressions—a smile for praise, a frown for disappointment.

Body Expressions

Communication using your body (arms and hands) is effective, too. Have you ever noticed that when people are angry, they often cross their arms. Or if they are upset, they may put their hands on their waists. I think it is essential to be aware of what our body position is saying to others and what other's bodies are saying to us. Once again, when Jim Carrey says something, watch his body language. A master of the use of the body, he can use it to suggest excitement or disappointment. Imagine him as a coach—watch out, Bollettieri, Van der Meer, Braden. Here comes Carrey!!!

As coaches or parents we need to pay attention to how we use the body when we deal with young children. *Rule:* Your arms, hands, and the rest of your body can magnify the words and sounds you use when talking with children.

Mirror, Mirror

"Mirror, mirror" is a behavior in which a coach/parent mimics a player's physical and verbal characteristics in an attempt to make her feel more at home in the lesson. As the expression goes, "When in Rome, do as the Romans." Well, the same with people—have you ever looked excitedly straight into a child's eyes only to have her look away? Sometimes our confidence and enthusiasm can intimidate young children. Introverted kids may avoid eye contact or glance back only occasionally. Often their body language is reserved, and they may speak in little "roller coasters" of uncertain tone. On the other hand, extroverts are often full of energy and very vocal. To mirror a player's behavior you must *subtlety* copy it physically and verbally. If the child is timid and small in stature, try and make yourself as small as you can. If the child's voice is soft and frail try to speak using a similar tone. It can be intimidating to use a powerful, loud voice with such a child. The *goal is to be able to communicate*—the more comfortable the student the better. *Rule:* It is important to identify children's psychological or emotional characteristics in order to communicate fully.

BUILDING RAPPORT

Name Tags (Nicknames)

Nicknames are personalized names created for people who are special to us. They take time and thought to create, and kids who get them feel lucky. I recommend giving players nicknames that are positive and complimentary rather than sarcastic and negative.

Using nicknames as a tool has two purposes. Giving a student a nickname can help you remember and distinguish him in a large crowd of people. Second, and more important, it helps make the student feel special. It should be easy to think up nicknames for students you have been coaching for some time. It can be based on a student's personal traits, repetitive sayings, something he loves to eat, something she always does, maybe his size, perhaps an anagram of her name. As examples, here are some of the nicknames I have used for some of my most notable students. Laura: Nooner, Sean: Seen, Michael: Joker, Ashley: Ash, William: Willie, Nargues: Narly Girl, Andy: Mang, Willow: Tree, Vivian: The Gun, Simone: Pooters, Sanjay: Burrito.

REQUIRED PHYSICAL QUALITIES

Motor-skills training must start at a young age if neuromuscular potential is to be fully developed as an adult. As Richard Schönborn, a biomechanics specialist associated with the German Tennis Federation says, it is important to be able to work within physical growth windows or a child may never reach his full potential in any physical area. It is important to participate in exercises that involve various qualities needed to play a well-rounded game of tennis. The following is a list of qualities that are used in the games presented in this book. Two examples of games using each quality are provided.

Anticipation: predicting what will occur by observing and gathering information to hypothesize an outcome, e.g., where the ball will be hit or what kind of ball will be hit. Games using this are Bubble Compass and Timber.

Balance: the act of controlling the center of gravity, whether by manipulating stances, or controlling body angles in positions such as leaning, crouching, or bending. Games using this are Bodybuilder and Body Parts.

Biomechanics (segment use): the use of the body parts independently or in conjunction with other parts. This is any physical movement performed in a game.

Coordination: the use of body segments so as to produce an intended, expected, or desired action, such as kicking, striking, or throwing. Games using this are Color Blast and Wrong Way Is the Right Way.

Dynamic balance: moving while maintaining balance. Games using this are Rope Them Up and Helicopter.

Reaction time: the time required to respond to a stimulus. The faster a child reacts the more time he'll have to perform a desired action. Games using this are Surprise and Kaboom.

Speed: how quickly a player can move around the court. Games using this are Spelling Spooks and Run for Your Life Tennis.

Static balance: balance when the body is still. Games using this are Stone Skipper and Chicken Pox.

Visualization: using a "cognitive map" or the imagination to see the outcome of an event before it happens. Games using this are Lighthouse and Lights Out.

GAME SKILLS

Each game is meant to develop specific tennis skills or techniques. Some will develop multiple skills.

Backhand grip: Place the index knuckle on top bevel of the racquet handle and rest the hand on the frame. For *two-handed backhands*, simply use the forehand grip (see below) and place the free hand above and directly in contact with the already positioned hand.

Centering skill: Contacting a tennis ball in the middle of the racquet's string bed.

Discovery: The use of self-experimentation and creativity when finding solutions to problems. Kids like puzzles, and they can often solve problems without adult help.

Forehand grip: Pick up the racquet and pretend to shake hands with the grip; this demonstrates the grip used to hit forehands.

Serve grip: Lay the racquet flat on the ground. Then pick up the racquet. Most of the hand's mass should be behind the handle so that there is stability when the racquet contacts the ball.

Guided discovery: Using clues provided by a coach to help students solve problems.

Juggling: Bouncing tennis balls on the racquet face either before or after the ball bounces on the ground.

Self-rally groundstroke: Using a racquet to hit a ball 5–10 inches above waist height then allowing the ball to bounce to the ground. A *continuous self-rally groundstroke* is the repeated hitting and bouncing of the ball on the ground. A forehand or backhand grip can be used.

Self-rally volley: Using a racquet to hit a ball 5–10 inches above the racquet then immediately hitting the ball up again without letting it touch the ground. In a *forehand volley* the palm of the racquet hand is facing toward the sky. In a *backhand volley* the back of the palm faces the sky.

Passing: Pushing, hitting, rolling, tossing, or exchanging a ball to or with a partner.

Projection: An action that makes an object travel. By performing a passing, rolling, hitting, or throwing action, a ball can be moved toward an intended target.

Reception skills: Before a ball can be hit, it must be received. Players work on receiving balls by performing movement in a certain way, preparing the body, or getting the racquet back before the ball arrives.

Rallying: Keeping a ball in play by alternating the same type of ball with a partner (e.g., same arched trajectory, same speed, etc.). Each player attempts to keep the ball in play, not to beat the other player. Competitive rally games will allow players to hit balls away from opponents, who will therefore have difficulty returning them.

GAME CATEGORIES

Some games require only one of the skills listed in the categories below, while others will call for several.

Self-rallying skills: In these a student will use a ball, a racquet, or the two in combination.

Reception skills: These skills will call for different ways of receiving a ball, at different planes, with and without movement, using hands and a racquet. Some games will use the hands, while other games will use a racquet.

Projecting skills: These skills will require that a student projects balls using the hands or a racquet when pushing, redirecting, tossing, throwing, blocking, and hitting.

Rally: Using control to exchange a ball with a player(s), with or without an obstacle.

Team games: These will promote teamwork, cooperation, and communication to reach a goal.

Miscellaneous: Tips and other tricks to make games more fun and interesting, along with games that combine several game categories.

GAME COMPONENTS

Each game includes the following topics.

Object: Developmental objective—The skill to be developed will be stated here.

Focus: Technical focus—The specific body part(s) to be used to execute the object will be designated.

Stroke: The strokes listed will indicate which strokes are developed in this game. Many games will allow various strokes to be used, but it is best to use one at a time. Some games require the use of multiple strokes.

Players: The number of players called for to play the game comfortably. Most games can be played with fewer players.

Equipment: All materials needed in order to play each game will be listed. If specified pieces are not available to you, of course you can substitute similar ones.

Setup and Game: A story or reason for playing the game. Using a theme or role-playing in a game makes it possible to deemphasize the technical or tactical side of the drill.

DIFFICULTY LEVELS

Within each game a coach or parent can add or remove components to increase or decrease the difficulty level.

To change the difficulty of a game, a coach or parent can change the **choice of stroke** in order to make a specific game more or less challenging. Generally speaking, strokes that require self-rally tasks are easier than those calling for partner-rally tasks. Following is a short list of skills/strokes ranging from least to most difficult:

Suggested progression of strokes *for each stroke*

It is recommended that the various tasks be taught in the following progressions. However, some players may excel at one stroke task and have difficulty with another. Therefore it is important at times to test players' abilities with more challenging tasks in order to check their progress and make adjustments in planning. If coaches, teachers, and parents do not test skill levels, players may spend unnecessary time on skills already acquired.

Groundstrokes (forehand and backhand)

1. Self-rally groundstroke pushing skill
2. Self-rally continuous centering skill (no bounces)
3. Self-rally juggle groundstroke
4. Self-rally continuous juggle groundstroke

5. Groundstrokes from a self-feed over an obstacle (net)
6. Groundstrokes from a coach feeding
7. Groundstrokes with a partner hitting groundstrokes
8. Groundstrokes with a partner volleying
9. Groundstrokes with a partner serving

Volley (forehand and backhand)
1. Self-rally juggle volley
2. Self-rally continuous juggle volley
3. Volley from a self-feed over an obstacle (net)
4. Volley from a coach feeding
5. Volleying with a partner volleying
6. Volleying with a partner hitting groundstrokes

Lob (forehand and backhand)
1. Self-rally juggle lob
2. Self-rally continuous juggle lobbing
3. Lob from a self-feed over an obstacle (net)
4. Lob from a coach feeding
5. Lob from a partner hitting groundstrokes
6. Lob from a partner hitting volleys

Overhead
1. Overhead from a self-feed
2. Overhead from a coach feeding
3. Overhead from a partner lobbing

Serving

1. Serving without an obstacle (net)

2. Serving with an obstacle (net)

3. Serving with increased distance from the obstacle (net)

The following is an example of a group of tasks chosen from various stroke progressions to be taught to a player in a lesson. Use the games section of the book to choose games that can accommodate the tasks.

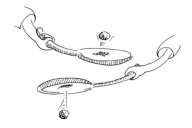

For example:

1. Self-rally continuous juggle groundstroke

2. Self-rally continuous juggle volley

3. Self-rally continuous juggle lobbing

4. Overhead from a self-feed

5. Serve without an obstacle (net)

Once categories and strokes have been determined other **difficulty options** can be added or removed to make games more suitable for children—such as using (from least to most difficult):

1. Large area targets (both service boxes)

2. Smaller targets (Hula Hoop)

3. Adding movement (requiring the player to incorporate movement)

4. Specific movement (requiring movement such as cross-over steps, shuffle steps)

5. Feeds that move the student around the court

6. Feed the ball with more pace, actual ball speed is faster

7. Quicken the interval of balls being fed

8. Feed the ball with some type of spin

If all this seems too complex, I suggest that you just jump right in, read the game, and use it. Through simple observation, and some trial and error, you will find out which games are most enjoyable and suitable for your students and children. There are no rights and wrongs, as long as there is fun in the games.

FORMATIONS

When using the games, there are many ways of positioning kids that can result in an exciting and full-participation fun time. I believe in *maximum participation* all the time. For many years coaches have said it's best to maximize participation when teaching young kids, and I think that's correct. And lately many professionals are using fewer line-up formations when teaching. Great job! But, I also believe that there are plenty of times when a line-up formation can *add* excitement to a game. I've seen the reactions and facial expressions of kids placed in team lines waiting for their turn. All of them are completely focused on the child at the front of the line. It's almost as if they were hitting each shot themselves.

Bottom line: *participation does not mean just always hitting a ball. It also means spirit and team spirit.* Of course high-performance, older kids need to hit as many correct repetitions as possible. But for younger, less experienced kids, the use of split lines or medium-size single lines can get the energy and excitement flowing.

PLANNING LESSONS

One-hour group lesson can be structured like this:

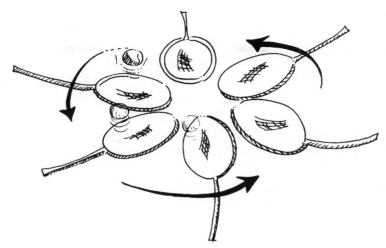

WARM-UP and explanation of the themes of the lesson: 5–10 minutes.

MAIN BODY of Games that incorporate the selected themes: 20–40 minutes.

COOL DOWN with stretching and a wrap-up of the day's lesson: 5–10 minutes.

The lesson plan suggested above is only a suggested format. There is no right or wrong way to use the games in this book. Be as creative as possible; almost any game can be played at a level appropriate to the kids' skill levels. During any one session, it's a good idea to play one or two from as many categories as skill levels permit. As a general rule, if the children are having fun, the lesson is a success, and the kids will want to play tennis in the future. Even if a player's skill level is low, if she's having fun, she'll want to keep playing. With practice, her skills will improve. Fun can make acquiring the most tedious skill seem exciting.

After observing how your students play the games, you can decide which direction is best to take, and select appropriate follow-up game(s). Generally speaking, absolute beginners will most enjoy self-rally and then projection games, but team games are always favorites because of the excitement of achieving group goals. Accomplished players will probably want to work on categories such as rally with a partner or projection/reception skill games. Once the games become familiar, players can return to old favorites without having the rules explained. You will notice kids asking to play specific ones and you will observe lots and lots of fun!

Successive lesson plans should be based on two factors: fun and effective performance indicators. If the kids had fun playing the games in the previous lesson, you can bet that they will be eager to play games in the next lesson. If the skill levels exhibited by the players were very low the same game(s) (or others in the same skills category) should be replayed.

GAMES! GAMES!
AND MORE GAMES!

SELF-RALLY GAMES

ROADBLOCKS

Objective: To develop control using a ball and racquet while performing centering and hitting skills.

Focus: Using the hand and forearm to control racquet action while moving.

Stroke: Centering skills, self-rally volley, self-rally groundstroke

Players: 6+

Equipment: Racquets, balls

Setup and Game: Players line up along the baseline and race to the net while centering the ball, doing a juggle volley, or a juggle groundstroke.

On the command "Go," players (cars) rush from the baseline to the net. The last player to reach the net becomes the roadblock. He must perform the centering or juggling while remaining in the middle of the playing field. The roadblock's job is to attempt to slow down or partially block the cars as they move past by standing in front of them. Each time the group of cars race to the opposite end of the playing field, the last person takes on the role of another roadblock. The game continues until only one car remains.

TAPEWORMS

Objective: To develop control using a ball and racquet while moving to avoid others.

Focus: Using the hand and forearm to control racquet action while moving left and right and crouching and ducking.

Stroke: Centering skills, self-rally volley, self-rally groundstroke

Players: 5+

Equipment: Racquets, balls, masking tape

Setup and Game:
Attach a three-inch loop of masking tape between each participant's shoulder blades. While performing a centering skill or juggle stroke, participants try to grab with their free hand the masking tape from other player's backs. The last person left with masking tape on his or her back wins.

If a player drops or loses control of the ball while performing a task, he or she must pick up the ball, place it in the middle of the string bed, and count to ten out loud while remaining stationary. Obviously, those counting are at greater risk of losing their tape. After ten seconds, they may resume taking tape off other participants' backs.

SECRET MINES

Objective: To develop control using a ball and racquet with some slow movement.

Focus: To use the hand and forearm to control the racquet.

Stroke: Centering skill, self-rally volley, self-rally groundstroke

Players: 8+

Equipment: Racquet, balls

Setup and Game: Players use any self-rally tasks, e.g., juggle groundstroke or juggle volley, while walking through a "minefield," extending from the baseline to the net, consisting of players sitting cross-legged on court. Some of the mines are designated active or inactive before beginning play. Only the mines themselves will know who has what designation. Active mines can explode. Inactive mines can be safely walked past.

To start the game, players walk from the baseline toward the net; mines are scattered on the way. Players walking through the mines do not know which ones are active and which ones are inactive. In order for players to make their way from the baseline to the net, they must walk in front of a mine and then wait to see whether mine shouts "KABOOM!" or "SAFE!" If the mine is active, then that mine and the player who activated it move to the sidelines.

If a mine is inactive, a player can go past it and move on to another mine as he or she attempts to make it through the field. As more and more players go through the field, the path to the other side of the field becomes clearer as active mines blow up and move away. Winner is the last player on the field once all the mines have exploded.

COPS AND ROBBERS

Objective: To develop various self-rally skills such as juggle volley or juggle groundstroke.

Focus: Centering the ball on the string bed involving the forearm and hand.

Stroke: Centering skills, self-rally volley, self-rally groundstroke.

Players: 2+

Equipment: Racquets, balls, tennis court lines

Setup and Game: Ask players to imagine that the tennis court lines are highways. Some players are police, while others are robbers. On the signal "GO," the cops are to chase after the robbers. During the chase, all players are asked to center the ball or self-rally using a juggle volley or juggle groundstroke. On "GO," robbers are given a ten-second lead to hit the highways before the cops can chase after them.

Throughout the chase, all robbers have to make a "VROOOM, VROOOM" sound while all cops make the sound of a police siren. If a robber mishandles a ball, it must be picked up and the robber must return to the spot where the ball was mishandled and perform five consecutive hits with the racquet and ball in the air before he is able to move again. If one of the police mishandles a ball, she, too, must perform a self-rally. If the skill level of the children does not allow them to perform continuous self-rally skills, they must retrieve the ball and count to five seconds out loud.

If one of the police touches a robber, the robber is placed in "jail" immediately. Jail can be any area off the playing field. The game can have several winners; the policeman who catches the most thieves wins, and the last robber to be caught wins.

LIGHTHOUSE

Objective: To enhance anticipation and visualization through auditory skills; to develop self-rally skills.

Focus: Using the hand and forearm to control the racquet and ball. Work at different planes—e.g., sitting, standing, and on tiptoes.

Stroke: Centering skills, self-rally volley, self-rally groundstroke

Players: 4–20

Equipment: Racquets, balls

Setup and Game: In this game, participants take on the roles of boats, lighthouses, and rocks. The player chosen to be the lighthouse stands with his back to the net. The lighthouse makes a foghorn sound while juggle volleying or juggling groundstrokes. "Rocks" are scattered throughout the court area in front of the lighthouse. Players chosen as rocks are to sit on the court facing

away from the net. They make a swishing sound while juggle volleying or centering the ball. Boats are players walking backward from the baseline to the net. While walking backward, boats perform juggle groundstrokes.

Rocks are capable of sinking boats that either come too close or crash against them. Boats that come too close can be tagged by a rock, at which time the two players exchange roles.

The first boat to make it to the lighthouse without crashing or sinking wins.

RACE CAR DRIVER

Objective: To develop teamwork and self-rallying skills

Focus: Using the hand and forearm

Stroke: Centering skills, self-rally volley, self-rally groundstroke

Players: 10+

Equipment: Racquets, balls, tennis court lines

Setup and Game: A team of five players make up an imaginary car and driver. Two teams (cars) are needed to play, and they race around the court area. Cars line up at the baseline to begin the race. The driver, positioned at the center of the car, will decide how many juggle volleys each member of the team, including her/himself, is to perform. After each person bounces a ball a given number of times on the racquet (juggle volley), the ball is passed on to the next person, until every team member has done the same thing. The car and driver then take the same number of steps as juggle volleys performed. If a ball is dropped, each team member must repeat the juggle volleys before being able to move again. The car that makes it around the court area, back to where the race began, wins.

ROPE THEM UP!

Objective: To develop control over ball and racquet while performing centering and racquet hitting actions.

Focus: Using the hand and forearm to control the racquet action when a ball is centered on the stringbed.

Stroke: Centering skills, self-rally volley, self-rally groundstroke

Players: 6+

Equipment: Racquets, balls, rope or towel

Setup and Game: Two cowboys/cowgirls hold onto a piece of rope or the ends of a towel in order to coral a stampeding herd of cattle. The number of players who are cattle can be negotiated at the beginning of the game. Cattle, while trying to escape being herded, perform a task such as centering the ball, performing a continuous juggle volley, or performing a continuous juggle groundstroke. Tasks to be performed by individual cows can be assigned according to the player's skill level. If a cow drops a ball, he/she is to stand still and count out loud to five before being able to move again.

Cows are herded when the two cowboys/cowgirls are able to touch their racquets together. As cows are herded, they are removed from the playing area. Cowboys/cowgirls keep their rope or towel (lasso) at waist height when roping cattle. The cowboy/cowgirls who catch the most cattle win.

MR. WOLF AND THE TENNIS KIDS

Objective: To develop various self-rally skills, such as juggling volley or juggling groundstroke.

Focus: Use of forearm and hand for centering the ball or for hitting upward in a self-rally.

Stroke: Self-rally volley, self-rally groundstroke

Players: 4+

Equipment: Racquets, balls

Setup and Game: One player is given the role of wolf, and he or she must attempt to tag all the other players. The wolf stands in the middle of the court, on the service line, with her or his back to the other players. They are positioned in a line, off the court, on the same side as the wolf. This will be their home base. The object of the game is to pass the service line and reach home. The

player who reaches home first is
the winner and takes the place
of the wolf.

While trying to reach
home, the players perform a task
such as continuous juggle volley
or volley continuously whenever
they move forward or backward.
The wolf must also perform a task, similar to the other players.

To begin the game, the players call out "What time is it,
Wolf?" The wolf replies calling out a time, say five o'clock. Each
time the question is asked, and the wolf replies with a time, the
players take a step forward. However, at some point, when the
wolf feels that the children are coming closer to home, he or she
may call out "lunchtime," simultaneously turning around and
attempting to tag the other players. The other players try to rush
home where they are safe. Anyone tagged is out.

ZOO MANIA

Objective: To develop self-
rally skills at various heights,
using sounds and different
body positions.

Focus: To manipulate the
racquet in relation to the
body, while keeping the racquet head in control. Using
the hand and forearm to
center the ball.

Stroke: Self-rally groundstroke, self-rally volley

Players: 4+

Equipment: Racquets, balls

Setup and Game: Divide the players into two teams. Have the teams line up in two rows. Create an obstacle course using pylons or tennis bags. Ask players to juggle volley or juggle groundstroke while making animal noises and actions specified by the coach.

The first team to complete the obstacle course while performing the tasks and sounds wins.

GOTCHA

Objective: Self-rally, centering, and juggling skills.

Focus: Controlling the wrist movement by keeping it to a minimum and using the forearm joint to initiate the vertical hitting action.

Stroke: Self-rally groundstroke, self-rally volley

Players: 4+

Equipment: Racquets, balls

Setup and Game: Choose a person to be It. Decide on a self-rallying skill that players must do and begin to play tag.

When the person who is It tags another person, or if the ball drops, the person tagged or the person who is being pursued who drops the ball, automatically become It, along with the original It.

Last person tagged wins.

JUGGLING TAG

Objective: Self-rally, centering, and juggling skills.

Focus: Controlling the wrist movement by keeping it to a minimum, and using the forearm to initiate vertical hitting action.

Stroke: Self-rally groundstroke, self-rally volley

Players: 4+

Equipment: Racquets, balls

Setup and Game: Pick a person to be It. Decide on the self-rallying skill and play tag. All players, including the person designated It, have to engage in the self-rally skill chosen.

The person who is It attempts to tag the other players. Anyone who drops the ball, automatically becomes It along with the original It.

The game ends when all players have been tagged.

PASSSSS IT

Objective: To develop racquet awareness and exchanging skills.

Focus: Control of the racquet head using the hand and forearm.

Stroke: Centering skills, self-rally groundstroke, self-rally volley

Players: 4+

Equipment: Racquets, balls

Setup and Game: Players are paired off. An area is designated in which players will be asked to shuffle along toward a finish line. Pairs pass the ball back and forth using the racquet while moving toward the finish line. The winning team is the one that makes it to the finish line first.

CHICKEN POX

Objective: Reaction time, self-rally skills.

Focus: Using the forearm and hand to hit a ball upward, with or without a bounce.

Stroke: Self-rally groundstroke, self-rally volley

Players: 3+

Equipment: Racquets, balls

Setup and Game: Players stand or sit in a circle; all players have a racquet but only one has a ball. The player with the ball has "chicken pox," and starts a chain reaction of "pox" by performing a self-juggle volley, hitting the ball at least three times in row. The person to the right of the sick person then performs the same action. On the command "Go," the action is performed person by person until it makes its way around the entire circle, that is until all the players have chicken pox.

The object of the game is to pass the pox as quickly as possible. This can be timed with a stopwatch, if so desired.

SHIP AHOY

Objective: To develop various self-rally skills such as juggle groundstroke and juggle volley.

Focus: Using the forearm and hand to stabilize the racquet head to center balls, hitting upward, downward, or alternating.

Stroke: Centering skills, self-rally groundstroke, self-rally volley

Players: 4+

Equipment: Racquets, balls

Setup and Game: Ask the players to spread out over the courts. Each player should have a ball and a racquet. The coach is the captain of the ship, and the players are sailors. The captain introduces various skills by  issuing commands and then demonstrating the action that is linked to the order. Some possibilities follow. Be creative coaches.

"*Captains on board*" Salute, then center the ball on the racquet.

"*Submarine in the water*" Lie down and put one leg in air while still centering the ball.

"*Man overboard*" Center the ball or juggle volley and turn in a circle.

"*Swab the deck, matey*" Place the ball on the ground and push it back and forth.

"*Too much wine, sailor*" Pretend to be drunk, center the ball, and swagger back and forth.

"*Land ho*" Center the ball with the racquet above eye level.

DOUBLE TROUBLE

Objective: To develop coordination, juggling 2 balls simultaneously.

Focus: Using the hand to hit 2 balls upward after the bounce, or using the racquet with palm down or palm up to hit a ball upward or downward and then immediately hitting another ball, thereby juggling two balls.

Stroke: Self-rally groundstroke, self-rally volley

Players: 8+

Equipment: Racquets, balls

Setup and Game: Each player finds an area on the court, a safe distance from each other. Each player is given two balls. The coach gives a task for forehand or backhand, such as self-juggle volley or self-juggle groundstroke.

All players are winners in that they all try to beat their personal best scores. Scores can be counted from the signal Go given by the coach. The winner is the person who is able to juggle the longest. Option—score can be kept as the total number of balls hit.

RUNAWAY TRAIN

Objective: To develop centering skills with some movement.

Focus: Players use hand and forearm to control a ball on a racquet.

Stroke: Centering skill, self-rally groundstroke, self-rally volley

Players: 8+

Equipment: Racquets, balls

Setup and Game: All players will have a ball and a racquet. One player is designated as the "runaway train," and stands at the net

beside the center strap. All the other trains are asked to stand on the doubles sideline, half on one side, half on the opposite side, so that all are

facing each other. When the coach says "All aboard," the runaway train then yells "Choo choo" and the name of one of the players. The runaway train then closes his eyes for 10–15 seconds, during which time the called train tries to signal one of the trains on the opposite side of the track, without talking. Players must center ball on the strings of the racquet while moving or perform a self-rally task. If the train makes contact with the other he hurries to switch sides. During his run to the other side, the runaway train attempts to tag or touch the switching trains. If either is touched, they switch places. If the called train cannot contact another, he must move to the center of the court and try to evade the runaway train for fifteen seconds. If he is touched, they switch roles. If the ball is dropped by the switching trains, they are automatically "it." If the runaway train touches another train but drops the ball, the tagged train is still free. Otherwise, a tagged train is out and must sit down. The winner is the last train untouched.

ACES

Objective: To develop centering and juggling skills alone or with a partner, while moving.

Focus: Using the hand and forearm to control the ball on the string bed.

Stroke: Centering skill, self-rally volley, self-rally groundstroke

Players: 4+

Equipment: Racquets and balls

Setup and Game: Form two teams. Name one team the "Aces" and the other team the "Aced." Line both teams up in the middle of a playing field so they are standing on opposite sides of a dividing line.

All players will be asked to perform a skill depending on the skill level of the players such as centering the ball, bouncing the ball on the strings, juggle groundstroke, or partner exchange volley, or partner exchange groundstroke.

On Go, all the students perform the skill and they continue when the coach calls out either Aces or Aced. The group called then chases the other group and attempts to tag the other team's players before they reach a safety line, all still performing the skill chosen.

All tagged players are out. If balls are mishandled by players they are considered tagged. The teams are lined up again and names called until one team has tagged all the other team's players.

MOVE IT, BUD

Objective: To develop racquet and ball control while incorporating movement.

Focus: Centering skills when using a ball and racquet by controlling the use of the hand and forearm.

Stroke: Centering skill, self-rally groundstroke, self-rally volley

Players: 8+ (There should be an even number of players; if there is an odd number, the coach can play.)

Equipment: Racquets, balls

Setup and Game: Players line up in pairs, one in front and one behind, and they form a circle within a circle. There is one person who is It and one person who is being chased.

Give each player a racquet and a ball that must be centered or self-juggle volleyed. On the word Go, the player who is It chases the other. If It catches the one chased, then she wins the game. The person being chased can hide from the player who is It by running in and out of the circled pairs. The chased can run and stand in front of or behind a paired person. When this happens, the paired person's partner standing in the inner or outer circle becomes the chased and must avoid whoever is It by running.

FRUIT SALAD

Objective: To develop centering skills while performing multiple tasks using a racquet and ball.

Focus: Developing an impact point, using the forearm and hand.

Stroke: Centering skills, self-rally groundstroke, self-rally volley

Players: 8+

Equipment: Racquets, balls

Setup and Game: Players are divided into four teams. Each team will be given a task and a chant to repeat.

    Tasks
    Group 1—Bounce the ball without dropping it.

Group 2—Bounce down without stopping.
Group 3—Step side to side.
Group 4—Hit the ball in the air and catch it.
Chants
Group 1—Pears, oranges, lemon pie.
Group 2—Plums, plums-plums, plums, plums-plums.
Group 3—Red ripe cherries, red ripe cherries.
Group 4—Cantaloupe-lope-lope-lope, cantaloupe.

Each group performs the task and simultaneously chants its song. After each of the four groups has had a turn, the coach or designated person calls out "Fruit Salad," at which time all the groups perform their skills and repeat their chants at the same time.

TENNIS DUCK TENNIS DUCK TENNIS GOOSE

Objective: To develop racquet control when self-rallying with some movement.

Focus: Players will use the hand and forearm to achieve control.

Stroke: Centering skills, self-rally groundstroke, self-rally volley

Players: 8+

Equipment: Racquets, balls

Setup and Game: All but one duck sit in a large circle facing the center. Each duck has a racquet and a ball. The duck that is It walks around the outside of the circle performing a ball and racquet task such as self-rallying, performing a juggle, or groundstroke. At the same time, he or she must lightly tap each player in the circle on the head with her or his nonracquet hand repeating the word *"duck"* with each tap. The challenge arrives when a player is tapped "goose" rather than "duck". The person tapped "goose" stands up and tries to tag "It" before It can make a complete circle back to the spot where "goose" was tapped.

If the ball is dropped, then the person must stop and pick it up before continuing the chase.

Once It reaches "goose's" spot, "goose" becomes It, and the game continues.

THE HUNTER IN THE WOODS

Objective: To develop consistency when self-rallying.

Focus: Players will use the hand and forearm to perform strokes.

Stroke: Centering skills, self-rally groundstroke, self-rally volley

Players: 8+

Equipment: Racquets, balls

Setup and Game: One person, a player or coach, is designated the Hunter. The other players are then asked to line up along one end of the court and are told to balance a ball on their racquet and imitate the actions and sounds of animals told to each one by the coach.

The hunter calls out, "I'm the hunter in these woods."

The other players respond, "What are you hunting for?"

The hunter then calls out an animal name, say a moose.

The players then move from the end of the court to a predesignated area, attempting not to be caught by the hunter. The hunter captures the animal by touching it with his free hand. If the hunter drops the ball, the animal is free; if the animal drops the ball, he is caught.

The game restarts when all the animals have been caught. A new Hunter must then be chosen.

CRAZY SHOES

Objective: Self-rallying skills, centering skills, with some body movements.

Focus: Using the hands to maintain the balance of the ball.

Stroke: Centering skill

Players: 6+

Equipment: Racquets, balls

Setup and Game: Ask players to take off their shoes and put them in a pile. The coach should then mix up the shoes so that pairs are not easily found. Players are then asked to stand back from the pile. Their task is to center a ball on a racquet and on the word Go, to try to find their shoes and put them on without letting the ball fall off the strings.

If the ball falls off, they are out of the competition.

DUCKS

Objective: To develop self-centering and self-juggling skills, with or without a partner.

Focus: Centering the ball, using the hand and forearm while moving. Some projection and reception skills may be performed if partners are used.

Stroke: Centering skill, self-rally groundstroke, self-rally volley

Players: 6+

Equipment: Racquets, balls

Setup and Game: Players pretend they are ducks and must race straight to the other side of the pond while centering a ball on the racquet strings. The pond can be a designated space on the court.

Initially, players start in a row in a squatting position. They must waddle like ducks and quack out loud. The first duck, or pair of ducks, to reach the other side of the pond wins.

TRUCK DRIVER

Objective: Self-rallying skills, centering, with some movement, all at varying skill levels.

Focus: Using hand(s) to balance the balls on racquet, to develop body awareness at different heights such as when crouching, or standing on tippy toes.

Stroke: Centering skill

Players: 4+

Equipment: Racquets, balls

Setup and Game: Players pretend they are trucks and walk around the court clockwise, collecting precious cargo (tennis balls).

They must collect six pieces of cargo.

Once six pieces are collected, the precious cargo can be transported home. Home is a preselected space on the court.

If cargo (a ball) is dropped, the truck driver must drive back from where she had come, now driving against oncoming traffic.

The driver with the most cargo delivered wins.

BATTLING KNIGHTS

Objective: To develop centering skills and hand-eye coordination.

Focus: Using the hand to balance balls in the middle of racquets. Using the nondominant hand to hit balls off racquets.

Stroke: Centering skill

Players: 4+

Equipment: Racquets, balls, paper towel tubes, or empty tennis

ball containers, grassy area is preferable

Setup and Game: Players pretend to be either horses or knights. The knights pair themselves up with a horse. Horses piggyback knights who balance a ball on a racquet string bed. Each horse and knight represent one team.

Each team's goal is to knock the balls from the knights' racquets. Knights are to carry a paper towel tube or empty tennis ball container in their nondominant hand. This is what they will use as a jousting lance.

The pair that manages to keep the ball on the racquet strings wins.

MARCO POLO TENNIS

Objective: To develop self-rally skills, auditory skills, and improve visualization.

Focus: Players use hand and forearm to control racquet and ball. There also is a focus on listening skills and visualizing through sounds in locating other players.

Stroke: Centering skill, self-rally groundstroke, self-rally volley

Players: 6+

Equipment: Racquets, balls, blindfold (scarf)

Setup and Game: Have players spread themselves out over the court, choosing one player to be It. Blindfold the person chosen as It. All other players will have one ball and a racquet.

Each player must bounce the ball on the racquet or perform a centering skill with the ball and racquet, as directed by the coach. Whenever It calls out "Marco," all the others must yell out "Polo" in response. The blindfolded person must attempt to tag the players by listening to their calls, the balls' bounces, and by visualizing.

Players are not allowed to move for ten seconds once "Marco" has been called out. If a player drops a ball he must automatically call out "Polo," even if "Marco" was not called.

WIZARD

Objective: To achieve realizable tasks and to encourage creativity in tennis skills work using a ball and racquet.

Focus: Skills can range from bouncing the ball a specific number of times to hopping on one foot and bouncing the ball on the stringbed. Focus points related to the tasks.

Stroke: n.a.

Players: 4+

Equipment: Racquets, balls, net at times is needed

Setup and Game: Each student has the chance to become the "Wizard." Players use their own imagination to create any type of game using a racquet, ball, or both. To gain the title of Wizard, players ask each other to perform various tasks such as hitting a specific target. For every task performed, a player is awarded one letter from the word *wizard* until the whole word is spelled out. The title Wizard is awarded to any player who wins all six letters.

NOAH'S ARK

Objective: Various skills of self-rallying, centering, juggle volley, or juggle groundstroke.

Focus: Relates to coach's tasks. Using hand and forearm to control a ball when performing various skills.

Stroke: Various

Players: 6+

Equipment: Racquets, balls

Setup and Game: One player is designated "Zoo Keeper" and the other players are animals. Each animal performs a specific skill given to her by the coach. There are two players assigned per each animal task. Animals spread out over the playing area, performing their different skills. The Zoo Keeper stands with his back to the animals while the tasks are being given out, and the animals are dispersing in the play space.

On the word "Go," the animals perform their tasks while the Zoo Keeper turns around, and pairs the animals who are performing the same tasks. As the animals are paired, they sit down.

The coach times how long it takes the Zoo Keeper to complete the pairings.

Each player should have a turn as Zoo Keeper. The winner is the Zoo Keeper with the fastest pairing time.

BIG HOOPS TENNIS

Objective: To develop self-rally skills bouncing a ball downward using a racquet, passing and receiving a ball from a teammate.

Focus: Using the hand and forearm to bounce a ball repeatedly downward. Using the hand to toss the ball into a basket.

Stroke: Self-rally groundstroke, future overhead, and serving action development

Players: 4+

Equipment: Racquets, balls, 2 boxes or elevated nets

Setup and Game: Players are divided into two teams who play a game of basketball using a tennis ball and tennis racquets. A box or elevated net is positioned at the two ends of a court.

Dribbling is performed with the racquet, bouncing the ball downward. Shooting is performed by throwing the ball with the hand into the baskets.

The team with the most baskets wins.

KNOCK DOWN THE GUARD

Objective: Anticipation with respect to the trajectory of the ball toward its intended target. Direction control when rolling or hitting balls is also worked on. Centering skills and movement.

Focus: Using the racquet to push or drop-feed hit to a target. Self-rallying juggling skills are performed using the hand and forearm by others.

Stroke: Push groundstroke from a ball on floor, optional self-rally skills

Players: 4+

Equipment: Racquets, balls, big plastic bottle or can

Setup and Game: The players are lined up along the doubles sideline as a starting point, and the guard will stand by the net parallel to the can and facing the base-line. The goal is to hit the can with a ball by pushing it or hitting it with a racquet. Each player is given a shooting number so that there is an order, and each has three chances to hit the target. If she hits it she earns a point and is free to jog to the other side with no worry about being tagged. If she misses, all the other players must run and cross the other doubles line while avoiding the guard who attempts to tag them. Players are allowed to move as soon as they think the ball will not hit the target. But if a player moves before the ball has passed the can and the can is hit, that player is out of the game. The guard can tag all players once the ball has crossed a line that is drawn one foot from the can. If he touches anyone, they are out of the game, or they can switch with the guard. The winner is the player with the most points or the first to get nine points. The player with the lowest score is the It for the next game. Players who are not shooting to knock down the guard may be asked to perform self-rally skills when moving to the safe line.

GUARD DOGS

Objective: To develop centering skills when using a racquet and a ball, with some movement.

Focus: Using the hand and forearm to control the angle of the racquet face. Centering the ball in the middle of the racquet strings will ensure a steady true bounce. Options can be to ask players to self-volley or self-groundstroke.

Stroke: Centering skills, self-rally volley, self-rally groundstroke

Players: 8+ (can be played with 3 and coach)

Equipment: Racquets, balls, tennis court lines

Setup and Game: The players are divided into two equal teams;

one is designated the ferocious dogs and the other the mail carrier. The mail carrier must try to deliver the mail by climbing over the fences (walking each tennis court line). They take turns trying to get to the house, which is at the other end of the tennis court.

Mail carriers start at one baseline and must work their way to the other side baseline. If a mail carrier can get to the net and touch any part of it, then he can slowly and safely walk to the other side and then, at his choice, can attempt to pass the rest of the guard dogs.

The guard dogs are to wait on each tennis court line. Guard dogs one and two are on each service line, and guard dogs three and four are on each baseline.

All players must self-juggle volley or self-juggle groundstroke continuously. If a mail carrier is touched by a guard dog then she must go all the way back to the post office (back fence starting line).

The team of mail carriers can all leave at the same time, or at intervals. They have six minutes to deliver as many letters to the house as possible, after which time the roles switch. The team with the most letters delivered wins.

SPIES

Objective: To develop self-rallying skills, recognition and observation skills, with some movement.

Focus: Using a racquet and ball to develop various self-rally skills. Movement is used to catch spies and to evade federal agents.

Stroke: Self-rally groundstroke, volley and various self-rally volley, center skills, combinations of strokes.

Players: 8+

Equipment: Racquets, balls

Setup and Game: Divide players into two teams. One team becomes FBI agents and the other team becomes spies.

Each player on the FBI team is given an action or task to perform that corresponds to an action or task performed by someone on the spies team.

The job of the FBI agents is to find and tag the spy who is performing the same action as she is. The spies , on the other hand, are to avoid capture by the FBI agents.

To begin the game, each team is asked to line up with their backs to each other. On the command Go, the teams turn around, and each member performs the assigned action or task. It is at this time that the FBI agents move in, attempting to catch the spy doing the same action or task that they are performing.

Once an FBI agent tags a spy, the agent and the spy caught sit down (return to the precinct). Time stops when the last FBI agent finds her corresponding spy. The time it took for all spies to be caught is recorded, after which the teams switch roles, and the players are given new actions or tasks to perform.

Ideas for skills:

1. Bounce ball once on racquet, then rest.
2. Bounce ball once on racquet, then tap ground with hand.
3. Bounce ball once on racquet, then say a word like "jello."
4. Bounce ball continuously in the air.

HAWAIIAN LIMBO

Objective: To develop ball control when the body is moved in an upright standing position.

Focus: Players center the ball on the string bed of a racquet while manipulating the body by bending backwards. Self-rally tasks can be used such as self-juggle, volley, or groundstroke.

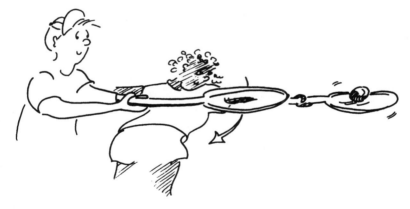

Stroke: Centering skills

Players: 4+

Equipment: Racquets, balls

Setup and Game: The coach will put her racquet straight out at shoulder height or higher. The players then move slowly, passing underneath the coach's racquet.

If a player drops his ball, he is out. After the line of players has passed under the coach's racquet, then the coach lowers her racquet.

This is repeated, with the coach lowering the outstretched racquet each time the whole line has gone under. The winner is the last player who can pass under the coach's racquet and still control the ball.

WILD CARDS

Objective: To develop various ball control skills while self-rallying.

Focus: The coach announces skills to be performed. The hand and forearm are emphasized.

Stroke: Center skill, self-rally groundstroke, self-rally volley

Players: 4+

Equipment: Racquets, balls, deck of cards, paper, pens

Setup and Game: Scatter players over the court. Give each player a ball and racquet. The coach deals out five cards, face down, to each player. Then the coach asks all the players to perform a self-rally task such as six juggle volleys in a row or to center the ball in the middle of the strings without touching the side of the racquet.

When a player successfully performs an action he can turn over his top card. The number on the card determines the number of points earned. For example, a card with the number five on it earns five points.

The coach then asks the players to do another task. After five rounds, the players total their points. The winner is the player with the most points. Cards that were not turned over are not counted. Picture cards are ten points including the aces.

CROOKED CAPS

Objective: Visual tag game with self-rally tasks. Perception and recognition skills.

Focus: Using the hand and forearm such as self-juggling downward or upward, or self-juggle volleying.

Stroke: Self-rally groundstroke, self-rally volley

Players: 6+

Equipment: Racquets, balls, hats, visors

Setup and Game: Players spread out over the court area with a hat positioned at their feet. The coach approaches each player and whispers "No" or "It." Anyone who receives an It command is to put his hat on any way but the normal way (e.g., sideways, backwards). Anyone given a No command puts his hat on the proper way.

On the command "Go," all players pick up their hats and put them on as instructed. All It players tag the other players to eliminate them from the game.

As soon as the first person is tagged, the round is over, and the process begins again. The process is repeated until three people are left, with one person It. If the It tags one of the two players within fifteen seconds, he wins. If the other players get away, they split the win.

TEAM GAMES

CAT'S TAIL

Objective: To develop centering skills and juggle skills.

Focus: Hand and forearm control; getting to know the racquet and ball in relation to the body.

Stroke: Centering skills, self-rally volley, self-rally groundstroke

Players: 8+

Equipment: Racquets, balls

Setup and Game: Players are placed on two teams. Each team forms a line. The person at the front of the line is the cat's head. The person at the end of the line is the cat's tail. The head of each team attempts to catch the tail of the opposite team.

To connect the players of each team, individuals hold on to the person in front of them at the waist with one hand, while holding a racquet with a ball in the center of it in the other hand.

The teams, without letting go of one another and without dropping the tennis balls, try to avoid having the tail of their team caught by the head of the other team. The team who catches a tail first wins.

If a ball is dropped, the team must freeze for a count of three.

CRICKET-BASEBALL TENNIS

Objective: To develop control when hitting a ball toward an intended area. To develop catching skills for hands and feet.

Focus: Tossing a ball at a target. Using a racquet to hit a ball to different areas; learning that the longer the backswing, the greater the distance the ball will travel.

Strokes: Groundstrokes, volley, throwing and catching skills

Players: 8+

Equipment: Racquets, balls, tennis court lines

Setup and Game: Two teams are to be formed. Each will have an opportunity to bat and to field. The boundaries used will be the two court halves.

Team A will line up along the doubles sideline. Team B will spread out over the field (tennis court). Each team will designate a pitcher to pitch underhand to the opposing team. Batters use their tennis racquets to hit the ball. Three strikes and a batter is out. Once out, a player sits down outside the playing area. If a player is able to hit the ball, the entire batting team then runs to the other side of the field to the doubles alley. Once there, they line up in their original order (minus players called out). For each player who reaches the other side without being tagged, a run is counted. If a fielder catches the ball in the air, the batter is out. If a fielder picks up a ground ball, he/she can tag any batting team player as they run to the sideline. While tagging, the fielding team may throw the ball back and forth to one another. When all the batters have had a turn, the teams switch positions.

THE LEANING TOWER

Objective: To develop reaction time and speed.

Focus: Players use explosive steps to develop speed and quickness; eye-hand coordination is also developed using the hand to catch the racquet.

Stroke: n.a.

Players: 2+

Equipment: Racquets

Setup and Game: Working in pairs, players stand two feet

apart. Holding the butt end of their racquet, each lets go of his or her racquet on the signal "Go" and attempts to catch the other person's racquet before it touches the ground.

A greater challenge is created by moving farther apart.

CHAIN REACTION

Objective: To develop teamwork with passing and receiving skills and minor projection skills.

Focus: Manipulation of racquet using arms and hands; creating hitting actions.

Stroke: Skills, groundstroke from self-feed

Players: 6+

Equipment: Racquets, balls

Setup and Game: Two or more teams form straight lines, each with a racquet at the front of the line. When the coach calls "Go," players pass the racquet back to the last person in line. The last person then runs to the front of the line and hits a ball to a specified target area.

This is repeated until all the players have had a chance to hit.

Other variations include passing the racquet between the legs, over the head, or around the waist.

STONE SKIPPER

Objective: To develop reception and projection skills.

Focus: Using catching and throwing skills, players use both hands to catch balls. The dominant hand is used to toss underhand and overhand.

Stroke: n.a.

Players: 8+

Equipment:
Tennis ball or
large light ball

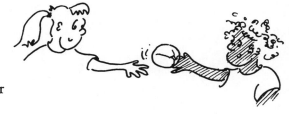

Setup and Game: Two teams are formed with each team placed opposite the other in a zigzag pattern. The coach places marks on the court using tape or chalk to show where players must stand.

A goal area is designated at one end of the playing space.

A goalie is placed just outside the goal. A balloon or light ball is passed back and forth to teammates who attempt to throw it into the goal. Players are only allowed to move one step in any direction. The team with the most goals wins.

RUN AROUND

Objective: To develop receiving and projecting skills.

Focus: Using body, arms, hands to create hitting actions, catching actions, with movement.

Stroke: Groundstroke, volley, centering skills

Players: 4+

Equipment: Racquets, balls, field, cones, or substitute items

Setup and Game: The coach creates two teams. One team will be up at bat while the other team plays the field. Set up two cones, fifteen feet apart.

The player at bat will feed himself and hit the ball anywhere within the court, however, the ball must hit the ground immediately. The ball cannot be hit as a line drive. If balls are hit over the surrounding fence, the player at bat is out. Once a player hits, she runs from cone to cone, touching them as she goes back and forth. Each time she touches a cone, a point is awarded. *Optional:* Have the runner center a ball on the strings while moving.

The fielding team tries to get to the ball as quickly as possible and then to throw it in to a player who is close to one of the cones. The fielding player then touches the ball to one of the cones, forcing the runner to stop running for points.

Once the entire team has batted, the next team is up to bat. The winning team is the one with the most points.

CANADIAN TENNISOCKEY

Objective: To develop pushing and rolling skills using a racquet and ball with some movement.

Focus: Using the hand to control the racquet head in order to push the ball toward teammates and the goal.

Stroke: Skills, self-rally groundstroke, self-rally volley

Players: 4+

Equipment: Racquets, balls, net area

Setup and Game: Set up hockey nets at opposite ends of the playing space and divide players into two teams. Players can push or pass the ball using only forehand or backhand grips, or they must bounce the ball, one dribble for every step they take. In order to shoot at the goalie, the player must perform a task immediately prior to shooting.

    The team with the most goals wins.

LIGHTS OUT

Objective: To develop communication skills, reaction time, visualization skills, and centering skills.

Focus: Players attempt to communicate to a player who is blindfolded. The blindfolded player works on centering skills and listening skills. All blindfolded players are asked to walk heel toe; absolutely no running is allowed.

Stroke: Centering skill

Players: 4+

Equipment: Racquets, balls, blindfold (cloth or handkerchief)

Setup and Game: Pair off kids into groups of two and divide these pairs into two teams. Each team is lined up well behind the baseline. In the first pair at the beginning of each team's line one member is given a racquet and a ball and is asked to center the ball while blindfolded. The other player will play the role of communicator and will speak to the blindfolded player telling him to step right, left, and so on. The goal is to get all blindfolded players to drop a ball into a four-foot-wide goal area at the foot of the net. Difficulty can be created by placing obstacles in each team's path. Once a player is able to drop off a ball into the goal, then the blindfold is taken off, and the two must run back to the next pair handing over the blindfold to the next player. The process is repeated again until one team has successfully scored all goals.

NOTE: penalties are assessed if the player who is blindfolded drops a ball and the seeing player picks up the ball and places it on the strings. If this happens, the blindfolded player must stand still and count to five out loud before moving.

BASEBALL TENNIS

Objective: To develop reception and projection skills.

Focus: Students learn direction control by using the racquet head to face (horizontal racquet angle) where the ball will be hit. The height will be controlled by altering the racquet angle to the sky. Throwing skills also will be performed. Reception skills are involved when catching balls with bare hands.

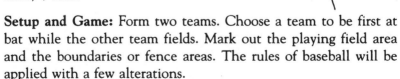

Stroke: Groundstroke

Players: 7+

Equipment: Racquets, balls, 4 bases

Setup and Game: Form two teams. Choose a team to be first at bat while the other team fields. Mark out the playing field area and the boundaries or fence areas. The rules of baseball will be applied with a few alterations.

Each member of the batting team will be given an opportunity at bat. If the ball is hit too hard and rolls past a certain line specified in the playing field, the batter is automatically out. The team with the most runs wins.

CHOPSTICKS

Objective: To develop racquet awareness and teamwork, with some movement.

Focus: Using the racquet as an extension of the arm, player's attempt to balance a ball between two racquet handles held side by side. Through experimentation, players will discover racquet positions that help balance the ball.

Stroke: n.a.

Players: 6+

Equipment: Racquets, balls

Setup and Game: Players pair up. Each pair holds their racquets by the head, using the handle end as chopsticks. They then place a noodle (ball) near the grip between the two rackets. The paired team walks a specified short distance to a drop area (bowl). The next teamed pair then goes over and performs the same task. The team with the most noodles in their bowl wins.

RIDICULOUS RACQUET RELAY

Objective: Coordination of different body parts.

Focus: Manipulation of body in order to transport objects from one place to another.

Stroke: n.a.

Players: 4+

Equipment: Racquets, balls (Optional: different types of balls)

Setup and Game: Form two teams, with two players on each team. The game is played as each pair attempts to pick up a rac-

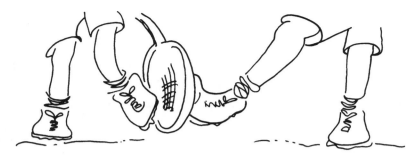

quet and ball and pass these to the other pair. The challenge is in finding a way to hold on to the racquet and ball with any other body part but the hands.

TEAM SPELLING SPOOKS

Objective: To support children's use of correct tennis terms.

Focus: Children will spell words associated with tennis in teams.

Stroke: Lob

Players: 4+

Equipment: Tennis balls, paper and pens

Setup and Game: Form two teams. Each team is to write down both easy and difficult words associated with tennis.

Each team assigns one player to whisper a word selected by the team to the coach, who will say the word out loud after hitting a tennis ball in the air.

A member from the opposing team must then attempt to spell the word in its entirety before the ball hits the ground, and then he hits the ball over the net.

A point is awarded for every word spelled correctly and for each ball hit over the net. The team with the most points wins.

The coach should hit the ball to a height proportionate to the difficulty of the word to be spelled.

BOOMERANG BALLS

Objective: Teamwork, projection, and reception skills.

Focus: Players will work on passing balls by rolling them using the hand, pushing with the racquet, or self-hitting using the racquet from a drop feed.

Stroke: Groundstroke, volley from self-feed

Players: 4+

Equipment: Racquets, balls

Setup and Game: Each player is given a partner. All pairs play simultaneously against one another. All pairs are at a starting line, shoulder to shoulder with their teammates. One member of each pair will be designated as the catcher and the other will be the running fielder. The catcher always stays on the starting line. Her job is to catch and throw back to the fielder. The fielder must move as far as he thinks the catcher and he can pass and catch the ball.

When the fielder thinks the catcher can get him the ball he calls out loud, signaling the catcher to pass the ball. Once the fielder catches the ball, he throws it back. It is only at this time that the fielder can move farther away. The winning team is the team that is able to pass, catch, and return the ball the greatest distance.

FRIENDLY FEUD

Objective: To develop team spirit, tennis education, self-rally skills, projection and reception skills.

Focus: Working with the ball using various racquet skills.

Stroke: Various skills

Players: 6+

Equipment: Paper, pens, racquets, balls

Setup and Game: Form two teams. Teams are asked to sit down facing each other in two lines that are three feet apart. Each team picks a captain to sit at the head of the line. When the coach calls "C'mon down and play the Feud," one member from each team, beginning with the captain, walks up and stands at the side of the coach. The coach then describes a task to be done. Following the description, a question related to tennis is asked. The player who knows the answer must perform the task successfully in order to give a response.

The team with the most correct answers wins.

ONE RACQUET RALLY

Objective: To develop directional control and maintain consistency.

Focus: Direction control is achieved by changing impacts in front and beside the body (horizontal racquet angle). Height is controlled by tilting the face of the racquet at impact(vertical racquet angle).

Stroke: Groundstroke, volley

Players: 4+

Equipment: Racquet, balls, net

Setup and Game: Pair off players into teams of two. Each team is given one racquet. Kings, Queens, or a King and a Queen of the court are assigned on one side of the net.

All challenger pairs are lined up ready to play against the top pair (Kings, Queens, or King and Queen). On Go, the ball is fed and the players play out the point as in doubles.

The catch is that the players must move as a team with each player anticipating the moves and shots of both teammate and opponents. When one team member hits the ball, she hands the racquet to her partner to continue the rally. The ball must be hit in an arc.

As an illustration of the kind of play produced, if a drop shot is hit, then the player will probably be off balance, and therefore the next logical shot would be the lob.

LOOK, NO HANDS!

Objective: To develop body awareness, creativity, and imagination.

Focus: Students use the body, arms, legs, knees, etc., to pick up balls and transport them to an intended area.

Stroke: n.a.

Players: 8+

Equipment: Balls

Setup and Game: Line up the students single file in two teams. Players pick up balls without using their hands and then deliver them to a drop area. The team with the most balls delivered in the area will win the game. Kids can use hands, knees, ankles, throat, elbows, and so on. The coach can designate a specific body part to use. The team with the most balls delivered to the drop area win.

REBOUND

Objective: To develop rally skills and an understanding of rebound.

Focus: To use the hand and forearm to create a downward hitting action, with some movement.

Stroke: Volley-type action, overhead-type action

Players: 2+

Equipment: Racquet, balls

Setup and Game: Players will be paired off and are to rally playing points using only one service box as the court boundaries. Therefore two matches can be played on one full court if there are four players. Players stand on opposite sides of the net. To begin a player must hit the ball down on his side of the net so that the rebound is high enough to clear the net and land on his opponent's side. The players can hit the ball downward only, but balls can be intercepted and then hit immediately back down on the player's side without allowing the ball to first land on the court. Points are won when a player fails to rebound the ball over the net and land it in his opponent's service box. The winner is the first person to gain 11 points. Players take turns starting each point.

TENNIS TEAM TENNIS

Objective: To develop consistency when receiving and sending various types of balls.

Focus: Teaching various ball controls, such as height, spin, speed, distance, and direction.

Stroke: Groundstroke, volley, overhead (hit with arc), lob

Players: 6+

Equipment: Racquets, balls, net

Setup and Game: The players are divided into two teams. Scattered formation is used to cover the playing surface (the entire court). The idea is to outrally the opposing team and force it into making errors.

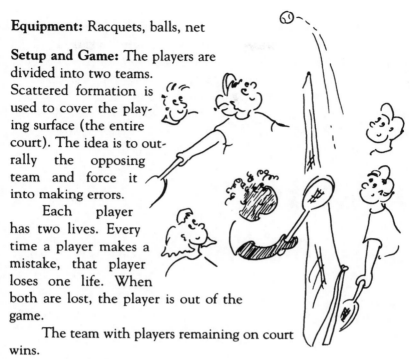

Each player has two lives. Every time a player makes a mistake, that player loses one life. When both are lost, the player is out of the game.

The team with players remaining on court wins.

NOTE: The ball must always be hit with an arc. The coach will feed the first ball, shouting out "Ball's in play," each time a new ball is fed.

POWER BALL TAG

Objective: Reception skills and projection skills when catching and throwing the ball to teammates. Tag variation.

Focus: Using throwing and catching actions with movement.

Stroke: n.a.

Players: 4+

Equipment: Ball(s)

Setup and Game: One player is named It and has the possession of the power ball (a tennis ball). When the player who is It touches another player with the ball, then both are It. By tossing the power ball back to each other, the Its can trap or corner free runners and then tag them, thus making them Its also. Therefore, there can be many people who are It. However, It can only tag free runners if they themselves possess the power ball. The winner is the last free person.

RUNDOWN

Objective: To develop hand-eye coordination when catching and tossing balls with movement. To develop quick change of direction movement.

Focus: Using the hands and forearms to catch balls and throw balls when moving. Using explosive steps to change direction as the middle man.

Stroke: Motor skills that will promote returning serve, volleying. Changes of direction when moving.

Players: 3+

Setup and Game: Designate two players who are the catchers and tossers and one player who starts in the middle of two bases. On "Go" the player in the middle runs from bag to bag; each time he touches one he scores a point. The two basemen who are guarding each bag must try to touch the player who is attempting to touch each bag. Basemen can leave their bag in an attempt to tag the runner in between the bags. But basemen can only tag the runner if they possess the ball. Therefore they toss the ball back and forth to each other in order to tag the runner. When the player in the middle is tagged he is out and becomes a baseman. The players take turns being the runner, and the winner is the person with the most bags touched after all players have had a turn as runner.

FLAG TENNIS

Objective: To develop ball control when moving. In addition, both projection and reception skills can be performed, depending on the skill level of the students.

Focus: Technical focus relative to strokes chosen by coach.

Stroke: Centering skill, self-rally volley

Players: 8+

Equipment: Racquets, balls, four strips of colored cloth six inches long and four plain white strips of cloth

Setup and Game: Divide the players into two teams. Give one team plain white strips and the other team colored strips. Have each team tuck the end of the strip into a belt loop or back pocket.

Have one team start at one end of the field. Tell them to try to get to the other team's goal. Each team has five chances to run with the ball centered on the racquet, ultimately to pass, or hit the ball into a goal area. If the ball is intercepted or picked up by the other team, then the offensive team loses possession and the new team attempts to score going the other way.

Whenever a strip is pulled from a running player who has the ball, or the ball is dropped, that player has to stop immediately. Then to prevent the opposing team from intercepting the ball she has to pass the ball on to a teammate.

OCTOPUS TENNIS TAG

Objective: To develop footwork, movement skills.

Focus: To move in conjunction with other players, using shuffling, running, walking, crossover steps.

Stroke: n.a.

Players: 6+

Equipment: Racquets, balls

Setup and Game: Choose one person to be the octopus. The game is played by having the octopus tag the other players as they run around or walk quickly away from him. Once a player is tagged she becomes part of the octopus, following the octopus's movements while also trying to catch other players. Every time a player is tagged, he becomes attached to the octopus. A single-person octopus must perform a self-rally skill; when there are two parts of the octopus, only one piece must perform a skill. When there are three or more pieces, only the outside pieces must perform tasks. All inside pieces of the octopus work on the specified footwork. Free, untagged players have to perform self-rally skills such as juggle volley. All players that are additional parts of the octopus do not perform any action with a racquet or ball.

TWIN TAG

Objective: Develop teamwork while moving and performing a self-rally skill.

Focus: Using the hand and forearm to control the balancing of the ball.

Stroke: Centering skills

Players: 4+

Equipment: Racquets, balls, ropes or pieces of cloth

Setup and Game: Pairs are selected and then are tied to each other with a bandanna or a piece of rope. The coach may tie up each pair by the ankles, arms, or the pair can simply hold hands. Coaches may want to add restrictions like absolutely no running, only walking. The game is a variation of tag only with a partner.

One pair of players is designated It. Only one member of each pair is to perform a skill assigned by the coach. The other member of the pair is the tagger. Whenever a pair is caught, they are It—they automatically become the tagger.

The last pair to be caught wins.

NIGHTHAWK

Objective: Centering skills, visualization, and communication skills with a partner.

Focus: Using the hand to center a ball in the middle of the strings. Blindfolded mice and hawks will listen to partners and visualize paths to follow. Have blindfolded players shuffle their feet along the ground so as not to trip on balls.

Stroke: Centering skills

Players: 4+

Equipment: Racquets, balls, handkerchief

Setup and Game: In the forest, hawks are searching for mice. The coach pairs off players so that one team are hawks and the other team are mice. From each team one member is immediately blindfolded. Balls are scattered all over the court, and the coach makes a path that is wide enough for players to walk safely through toward the net. The blindfolded mouse has a racquet and ball which is being centered. The communicator mouse starts telling the blind mouse where to walk to get to the net safe area. The hungry blindfolded hawk and his friend are not far behind, and are trying to find the mice. Mice start behind the baseline, and when the coach says Go, they try to go through the maze of balls to the net. The hawks soon follow. If a blindfolded player runs and does not walk, he is automatically out of the game. Any player who touches a ball with her foot must stand still and count out loud to five. A ball that is dropped off the racquet is replaced by the communicator and the blindfolded player must count out loud to five. The team of hawks that catches the most mice wins. Teams switch roles.

ALLEY OOPS

Objective: To develop tossing and catching skills.

Focus: Player tosses the ball in the air or bounces the ball to a teammate while attempting to stay away from an opposing player.

Stroke: n.a.

Players: 8+

Equipment: Balls, two goal areas

Setup and Game: Form two teams. Assign a goalkeeper for each team. One goalkeeper should be positioned in the corner of the add court while the other is positioned in the deuce court.

The two teams' players should position themselves anywhere, on either side of the net, in a scattered formation. A line marks how close to the goalie a player can stand.

To score a point, the ball is thrown to one of the goalies without the other team catching it. Teams try to throw a ball to their own goalie. When a goal is scored, the ball is given to the other team, and the passing begins again.

The winner is the team with the most goals.

CHAIN REACTION DOUBLES

Objective: To develop various strokes by using a team concept when serving, returning, and volleying.

Focus: Technical focus depends on strokes chosen.

Stroke: Serve, groundstroke, volley, overhead

Players: 4+

Equipment: Balls, racquet, net

Setup and Game: Put the players in doubles position, with one server, one returner, and one volleyer. The other players will be divided, in a safe waiting area, in each of the three positions. On the signal Go, the server has one chance to get the ball to the returner in the service box. The returner then has to return the ball over the net to the net person, who is volleying.

The volleyer must then hit the ball into a specific area. If all three players can successfully complete their tasks as a unit, then all three players will get one point.

Whichever player breaks the chain has to go to the end of the line at his particular station. The first person waiting, now has a chance to gain points.

If a player never makes a mistake, she continues to stay in that position.

RUGBY TENNIS

Objective: Teamwork, passing, and receiving skills.

Focus: Eye-hand coordination. Throwing and catching moving balls.

Stroke: Various

Players: 6+

Equipment: Tennis balls, grassy field (optional)

Setup and Game: Form two teams. Have each team take on a scattered formation on opposing halves of the field or court. The object of the game is to pass a ball back and forth by rolling it, bouncing it, or hitting it in the air to a teammate and then bouncing it into a goal area.

A player can take three steps before a pass has to be made, more than that and his team loses possession of the ball.

No hard hitting is allowed when shooting on goal.

CRICKET TENNIS

Objective: To develop projection and reception skills.

Focus: Projection will be performed by focusing on the racquet face at impact. Reception is performed by using the legs and hands to get behind balls and catching them.

Stroke: Centering skill, groundstroke, volley

Players: 6+

Equipment: Racquets, balls, pylons

Setup and Game: Set up two pylons approximately ten feet apart. The distance between the pylons can vary with the skill level of the players. Two teams are formed, one batting team and one fielding team. Every fielding team assigns one pitcher to stand in the infield.

Every batter must not only hit a ball to the outfield, but must also run with a ball on the strings, back and forth between two pylons, for points. Each time a player makes it to the other post, she is awarded a point for her team.

It is the fielders' job to catch the ball and throw it in to the pitcher in order to stop the player running. If the player is tagged by a fielder who has the ball, she is out. The teams switch positions once every team member has had a chance to bat.

The team with the most points wins.

SHOWDOWN HOCKEY

Objective: To learn how to project, push, roll, and strike balls on the floor.

Focus: Using forehand grips, backhand grips, and both hands to be able to pass, shoot, and receive balls.

Stroke: Pushing groundstroke, some catching skills and blocking skills

Players: 6+

Equipment: Racquets, balls, objects for net posts

Setup and Game: Players take on the role of hockey players. Two nets should be set up, about ten feet apart. One goalie is assigned for each team.

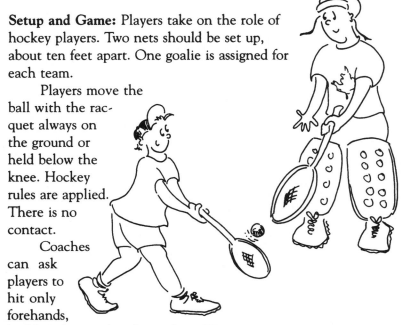

Players move the ball with the racquet always on the ground or held below the knee. Hockey rules are applied. There is no contact.

Coaches can ask players to hit only forehands, backhands, two hands, or feet. Winning teams can continue to play other teams, or several nets and field areas can be set up for pairs of players.

TENNIS RUMBLE

Objective: To develop self-rally skills.

Focus: Using the hand and forearm to lightly hit a ball upward, or downward, continuously. Coaches may use different tasks when self-rallying.

Stroke: Centering skill, self-rally volley, self-rally groundstroke

Players: 4+

Equipment: Racquets, balls

Setup and Game: Two equal gangs are created with each team creating a team name like Rebels or Warriors. All players have a racquet and a ball. Each team will have a gang leader. The coach asks one gang to choose another gang member from the other team to battle with. When the teams have finished selecting, they all line up face to face with their chosen opponent. There should be two straight lines of gang members facing one another. The coach announces a task to do such as self-volley rally using palm up, and then he says, "Rumble." The first gang member of each pair who cannot complete the task loses the mini-rumble and must immediately sit off on the side line. Eventually, there will be only one member of each mini-rumble standing. The coach then says regroup, and the teams meet among themselves again. The gang with the fewer players chooses who they want to do battle with. Any extra players are reserves, and they go into battle when a team member loses. The process is repeated over and over until one gang remains.

BOCCIE TENNIS

Objective: To develop projection skills controlling direction and distance when pushing or hitting a ball.

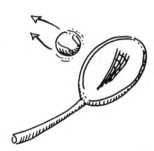

Focus: Lengthening or shortening the backswing, with and without a racquet.

Stroke: n.a.

Players: 4+

Equipment: Sixteen Balls (eight of one color, eight of a different color), one specially marked ball

Setup and Game: The coach divides the players into two teams. Each team receives eight balls. The coach rolls out one ball on to the playing field. The teams then take turns tossing or rolling their balls toward the special ball, trying to get their ball to stop closest to the special ball.

After the 8 balls are hit or rolled by each team, the first round is complete.

The team that got closest wins that round. The same process continues until a team earns four points.

SUPERKID

Objective: To develop rallying skills over a net, teamwork, and also communication.

Focus: To use proper racquet path and racquet angle to stroke the ball over the net. To use proper reception skills when receiving balls at varying heights.

Stroke: Groundstrokes, volley, overhead, lob, serve (optional)

Players: 8+

Equipment: Racquet, balls, net

Setup and Game: Each team attempts to out-rally the other by rallying a ball over the net into their opponent's court. If a player makes an error, such as hitting the ball into the net, the team member designated as "Superkid" can come to the rescue. Coming to the rescue means keeping the ball bouncing and then hitting it to a teammate or over the net. A team member, other than "Superkid," who causes the ball to roll on the ground is out of the game, and he or she must sit on the sideline unless Superkid saves the day.

The cry "Ball's in play" will start each point. The first ball cannot be hit out of the air. It must be hit from the first bounce. All balls must be hit in an arched trajectory. No smashes or drives are allowed. There should be a maximum of two "Superkids" assigned per team.

PROJECTION GAMES

TICK-TOCK CLOCK

Objective: To develop control when hitting a ball with a racquet toward an intended target. To develop self-rallying skills.

Focus: Controlling the racquet face and racquet path at contact, in order to control direction. Using the hand and forearm to center the ball when performing racquet and ball-juggling skills.

Strokes: Self-rally volley, self-rally groundstrokes, groundstrokes, volley

Players: 4+

Equipment: Racquets, balls

Setup and Game: Set up a target area on court. One player is asked to hit balls into this area. A second player juggle volleys or performs juggle groundstrokes; he or she is the human clock. When the clock has hit a certain number of balls in a row, then he or she calls out "Stop." The first player is then to stop hitting balls into the target area. The number of balls hit into the area are counted. The winner is the player with the most balls successfully hit into the target area.

FOUR ON THE FLOOR

Objective: To discover the relationship of distance to speed and to height of balls as they are sent to an intended target.

Focus: To achieve different heights, the racquet face is opened or closed. The speed of the racquet before impact varies as the length of the swing is changed.

Stroke: Groundstrokes, volley, serve with arc, lob from self-feed

Players: 4–16

Equipment: Empty basket, ball hopper, or milk crate, racquets, balls

Setup and Game: Place an empty basket in the middle of four lines of players. Each line is given a hopper of balls. The goal is to toss or hit the balls into the empty basket.

The team with the most balls in the basket wins. Variations can be introduced such as making sure that the ball bounces two times or three times before entering the basket.

BULL'S EYE

Objective: To develop control when hitting a ball toward an intended area.

Focus: To develop consistency through positioning the body—body is sideways, racquet face is open, use small racquet action, strive for a tapping feeling.

Stroke: Ground-strokes

Players: 2+

Equipment: Racquets, balls, net

Setup and Game: A triangle of balls is placed on the ground in front of the net as a target. Pairs of players then take turns trying to hit the target within an allotted time (three-minute rotations). If either player is not able to hit the target, each must take a turn dropping and hitting a ball toward the target. The player whose ball lands closest to the target wins.

The winning player then must find another player to challenge. The person with the most target hits wins.

To add a level of difficulty, obstacles can be placed in front of the target.

SIX SHOOTER

Objective: To develop control when hitting from various angles.

Focus: Controlling the racquet face and racquet path at contact in order to control direction.

Players: 2+

Stroke: Groundstrokes, volley, lob, serve

Equipment: Racquets, balls, net

Setup and Game: Six positions or stations are identified and marked around the court. These positions or stations are the spot from which each player hits balls toward a target. Every player has a chance to hit two balls from each position or station. Those not hitting are to count the number of times each player hits the target. Players have thirty seconds to hit as many of the twelve balls as they can.

SOCK IT TO ME

Objective: To develop a sense of distance and distance control when projecting an object.

Focus: Players will use underhand pendulum-like actions to toss sockballs over the net and into targets.

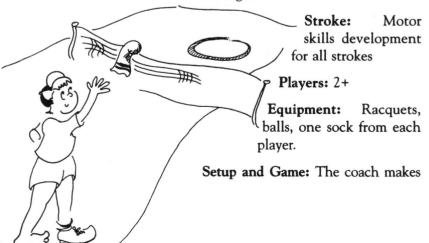

Stroke: Motor skills development for all strokes

Players: 2+

Equipment: Racquets, balls, one sock from each player.

Setup and Game: The coach makes

two equal teams and each team stands on the each service line facing the net. Targets are placed in each service box on each side of the court. The coach asks all the players to take off one of their socks and then to put the shoe back on. Stuff a tennis ball in the sock and now we have our weapons. On the signal Go, the players toss their sockballs to the opposing side, attempting to land them in a spatial target for points. Once all the sockballs are thrown, they are picked up and the process starts again. The team with the most points wins.

THROUGH THE TUNNEL

Objective: To develop direction control when pushing or rolling balls with a racquet.

Focus: Players will be asked to push balls using the racquet head into the tunnel (between the feet of other players).

Stroke: Pushing rolling balls, pushing ground-stroke

Players: 3+

Equipment: Racquets, balls

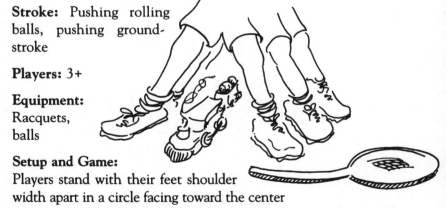

Setup and Game: Players stand with their feet shoulder width apart in a circle facing toward the center approximately two feet apart. They are the human tunnels. The conductor is a player who stands in the middle of the circle with a basket of balls. On the signal when the coach yells "All Aboard!" the conductor starts loading the passengers (balls) onto the imaginary trains and speeding them off to their destinations. The coach yells "End of the Line!" After, for example, thirty seconds, winner is the person who hits the most balls through the tunnels.

BATCATCHER

Objective: To develop distance control using height and speed and direction control when rolling, bouncing, or tossing balls to a target area.

Focus: Depending on the kids level of skill, the coach may ask the player to use an underhand or overhead tossing action to land balls to the batcatcher. Players self-drop feed themselves and use a racquet to hit balls to the catcher with forehand or backhand.

Stroke: Self-fed groundstroke, self-fed volley

Players: 2+

Equipment: Racquets, balls, baseball glove optional

Setup and Game: Divide the players into two baseball teams. Each team is lined up beside each other and the batcatcher (the coach) sits in a crouched position on the other side of the net. The distance of the catcher to the net is close at first, then increased for difficulty. A basket of balls is placed in between both lines at the front. When the coach yells out Play Ball, the first player from each team picks up a ball and projects it toward the catcher for points. The catcher must be able to catch the ball(s) without moving from the crouched position. If the player hits a ball far from the catcher, no points are scored. The winning team is the team with the most points.

STRIKE IT RICH

Objective: To develop control when hitting a ball toward an intended area. To develop self-rallying skills.

Focus: Controlling the racquet face and racquet path at contact in order to control direction.

Using the hand and forearm to center the ball when performing racquet and ball juggling skills.

Stroke: Groundstrokes from a ball on the floor, self-rally groundstroke, or volley

Players: 4+

Equipment: Racquets, balls, empty tennis ball tins

Setup and Game: Players are given a specific skill such as bouncing the ball on the string bed a certain number of times. Once that task is completed, players earn the chance to "Bowl" and earn points. Tennis ball tins are used as bowling pins.

Players use their tennis racquets and tennis balls to knock over the pins. One point is awarded for each pin knocked down. The winner is the player with the most points.

KEEP IT OUT OF THE HOUSE

Objective: To develop consistency and the ability to change direction when rallying.

Focus: Controlling the direction of the ball by changing the impact altering it in front of the body and closer beside the body (horizontal face), putting the strings of the racquet toward the intended target.

Stroke: Groundstroke, volley

Players: 5+

Equipment: Racquets, balls, rope post or chairs

Setup and Game: Divide the tennis court into four squares. Place one person in each of the squares, and position the rest of the players in a line, off the court.

Name one player to be the top of the court. This person is to be the King or Queen of the game. He or she will start the ball in play.

The players must hit the ball after one bounce. The object of the game is to get the King or Queen out, or to be the King or Queen for the longest amount of time. If a player cannot keep the ball out of the court with one bounce, then he or she is out.

Each square is numbered one to four where 1 is the King; 2 is the Queen; 3 is the Prince; and 4 is the Dungeon.

TIC-TAC-TOE

Objective: To develop direction control.

Focus: Controlling ball direction by altering the impact of the ball in front of the body and closer beside the body, orienting the strings of the racquet toward the intended target.

Stroke: Groundstroke, volley, serve, lob, over-head (self-feed)

Players: 1+

Equipment: Racquets, balls, net, tar-gets

Setup and Game: "Tic-tac-toe, three in a row." Create three targets scattered over the

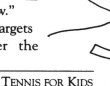

court. Two teams stand in the middle of the court, taking turns drop feeding themselves and hitting to the targets. Hitting targets allows a team to place an *x* or an *o* on the drawn tic-tac-toe lines. The winning team is the team that completes three in a row on the tic-tac-toe board. Teams can block another team's attempt at a three-in-a-row by hitting a target.

SHOOTING GALLERY

Objective: To develop direction control and depth control by hitting the ball at differing heights.

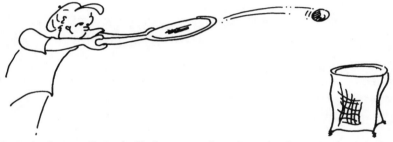

Focus: Controlling ball direction by altering the impact of the ball in front of the body and closer beside the body (horizontal racquet face), orienting the strings of the racquet toward the intended target. Learning how to hit the ball different distances by opening up the vertical racquet face at impact.

Stroke: Groundstroke, volley, serve (all self-fed)

Players: 1+

Equipment: Racquets, balls, net

Setup and Game: Players are lined up on the court, pretending to be hunters looking for targets to shoot at. Targets should be placed in corners of the court at different depths.

The object of the game is to hit as many targets as possible.

TERRIBLE TOPSPIN

Objective: To teach children how to create topspin or forward spin.

Focus: Each student is to self-feed and attempt to bring the racquet from below the intended impact to above the intended impact, simply from low to high.

Stroke: Groundstroke

Players: 4+

Equipment: Racquets, specially marked tennis balls, net (optional—a beach ball with multicolored markings)

Setup and Game: Have all students form two lines facing the same side of the net. Depending on the skill level, the students may need to start inside the service line then progress to the baseline. Watching the ball is important in order to see the forward spin.

UNBELIEVABLE UNDERSPINS

Objective: To teach children how to create underspin or backspin.

Focus: Each student is to self-feed and attempt to bring the racquet from above the intended impact ending below after impact, simply from high to low.

Stroke: Groundstroke

Players: 4+

Equipment: Racquets, specially marked tennis balls, net, (optional—a beach ball with multicolor markings)

Setup and Game: Have all students form two lines facing the net. Depending on the skill level, the students may need to start inside the service line, then progress to the baseline. Watching the balls is important in order to see the underspin or backspin.

SILLY SIDESPINS

Objective: To teach students how to create sidespin for emergency shots and to be creative. The spin will make the ball bounce into or away from the opponent.

Focus: Each student will be asked to brush the side of the ball like a clock face from 3 o'clock to 9 o'clock. The action is like a pendulum.

Stroke: Groundstroke

Players: 1+

Equipment: Racquets, and large, multicolored beachball(s)

Setup and Game: Place the players close to the net in single lines. The coach either asks players to drop feed themselves or to hand feed the beach ball to the students. The coach should comment on the spin that is created.

KNUCKLEBALLS

Objective: To develop a feel for the way the ball leaves the racquet; with this stroke there is little or no spin.

Focus: Before contact, at contact, and after contact the vertical racquet angle/face and the horizontal racquet angle/face are square and equal to one another, so that little to no spin on the ball is created.

Stroke: Groundstroke

Players: 1+

Equipment: Racquets, and large, multicolored beachball(s)

Setup and Game: Place the players close to the net in single lines and toss a large beach ball to them. After the bounce, the student will attempt to strike the ball, returning it with no spin.

HUNTERS

Objective: To develop direction control and depth control while hitting from challenging positions.

Focus: Controlling ball direction by altering the impact of the ball in front of the body and closer beside the body (horizontal racquet angle), orienting the strings of the racquet toward the intended target. Learning how to create depth by opening up the (vertical racquet angle) face at impact.

Stroke: Groundstroke, volley, serve (all self-fed)

Players: 1+

Equipment: Racquets, balls, net

Setup and Game: Players as "hunters," line up along the baseline ready to shoot targets. Targets are set up in predetermined areas by the coach.

Players are to hit the targets in order to earn points. Coaches ask hunters to hit from different body positions such as on tiptoe, squatting, on one foot bending over at the waist, sitting, standing with shoulders unbalanced, etc.

15, 30, 40 GAME

Objective: To introduce scoring and achieve distance and direction control.

Focus: Controlling ball direction by altering the impact of the ball in front of the body and closer beside the body (horizontal racquet angle), orienting the strings of the racquet toward the intended target. Learning how to create depth on the ball being hit by opening up the (vertical racquet angle) face at impact.

Stroke: Groundstroke, volley, serve

Players: 1+

Equipment: Racquets, balls, net

Setup and Game: Divide the court into three areas and ask players to hit to each zone. If the player hits the first zone, he/she is awarded the point "15". When four points are earned, the player wins one game. The player with the most games wins.

MAP

Objective: To introduce the court names and various positions, and to develop direction and distance control.

Focus: Controlling ball direction by altering the impact of the ball in front of the body and closer beside the body (horizontal racquet angle), orienting the strings of the racquet toward the intended target. Learning how to create depth on the ball being hit by opening up the (vertical racquet angle) face at impact. Explaining the scoring system.

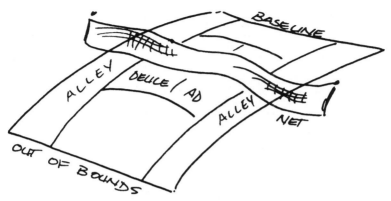

Stroke: Various strokes

Players: 1+

Equipment: Racquets, balls, net

Setup and Game: Players hit balls into specified areas of the court, such as the doubles sideline. For each area hit, a point is awarded. A player wins the challenge when the whole court has been hit.

MOVING TARGETS

Objective: Projection skills to develop directional control.

Focus: Controlling the direction of the ball by changing the impact of the ball, changing it in front of the body and closer beside the body (horizontal racquet angle).

Racquet strings should face the target at the time of impact.

Players: 3+

Equipment: Racquets, sponge balls, net (optional)

Setup and Game: Have players form three lines. Tell players to lightly shoot balls at the targets (the players or coach) moving around the court area.

A point is awarded for every target hit.

LIVES

Objective: To develop projection skills direction and height control hitting to a specific area from a self-fed ball.

Focus: To develop control height by opening the string bed at an angle facing the sky (vertical racquet angle), control direction by facing the strings at the target when making contact (horizontal racquet angle).

Stroke: Groundstroke, volley (from self-feed)

Players: 4+

Equipment: Racquets, balls, net

Setup and Game: All players stand on the service line, an arm's distance apart, racquet in hand. A basket of balls should be placed behind the service line. On the word "Go," the players pick up one ball and attempt to hit it over the net into a large area (single court). All players start off with nine lives. Each time a player is able to hit the ball over the net, she gains one more life. Each time she hits into the net, she loses a life. If a player loses all his lives, he then goes to the other side of the net and stands behind the opposite service line and attempts to catch balls. For every catch made a life is earned. When the player earns a life he is able to return to the other side, and he begins counting lives again. The player with the most lives gained within a specified time period wins.

HAWAIIAN HULA TENNIS

Objective: To develop projection skills after performing a complex trunk movement during a relay-type race.

Focus: Players will control height by opening and closing the racquet face at impact (vertical racquet angle), and they will control direction by altering the racquet face toward the intended target (horizontal racquet angle).

Stroke: Centering skills, self-fed groundstroke, self-fed volley, or coach can feed

Players: 4+

Equipment: Racquets, balls, net, two hula hoops

Setup and Game: Form two teams. Have the teams line up at the baseline. Each player has the hula hoop circle his waist, neck, arm, leg, or ankle in one complete revolution, and then he picks up one ball hitting it over the net into a target area. The team with the most balls in the target area wins.

WEIRD WALL CRAZE

Objective: Develop projecting skills.

Focus: Adjusting the racquet face toward the intended target (horizontal racquet angle). Using a hitting action to create some racquet speed for distance.

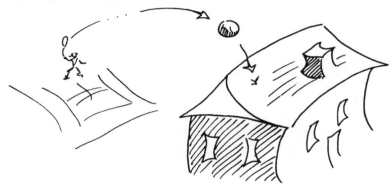

Stroke: Groundstroke, volley, serve, lob

Players: 4+

Equipment: Racquets, balls, net

Setup and Game: Players must hit a specific area on a fence, wall, or curtain before they are allowed to hit a ball into a designated area on the court for points. The winner is the person with the most points.

FLY ON THE WALL

Objective: To help students with direction and height control.

Focus: Players focus on hitting the ball with the racquet face facing the intended target (horizontal racquet angle). Height will be worked on by focusing on the angle of the strings in relation to the sky (vertical racquet angle).

Stroke: Groundstroke, volley (from a self-feed)

Players: 2+

Equipment: Racquets, balls, tape, paper, markers

Setup and Game: Before playing the game, draw large flies on pieces of paper and tape these to the fence or court divider.

Players line up a fair distance from the fly posters. Each player is then given a number of balls to be used to hit the flies. Points are awarded for direct hits.

As an option, sponge balls can be used, dunked in water so that they mark the flies that are hit.

MINIATURE GOLF

Objective: To learn projection skills such as pushing, tapping, and hitting balls using a racquet and ball.

Focus: Using the racquet as a golf putter, players are asked to use two hands, one hand, forehand, and backhands, to roll balls into the marked holes on the tennis/golf course.

Stroke: n.a.

Players: 3+

Equipment: White chalk, racquets, balls, paper, pencils

Setup and Game: Draw 8–10 golf holes over the tennis court to represent a golf course. Circles can be drawn to represent holes, squiggly lines can be used to represent the fairway, and squares with numbers in them can be used to mark the hole number.

Assign an individual to keep track of the number of strokes it takes each player to sink a ball. A ball is "sunk" when it rolls through a circle. The player with the lowest number of strokes wins.

This game can also be played in teams.

POOL SHARKS

Objective: To develop visualization and trajectory skills when controlling direction.

Focus: Using the butt end of a racquet, players attempt to push or hit balls to different areas of a tennis court pool table. Direction control.

Stroke: Pushing groundstroke skills

Players: 4+

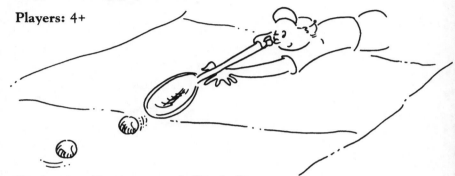

Equipment: Racquets, ten balls, chalk

Setup and Game: The big pool shootout is about to happen. Each player should have his own stick (the butt end of a racquet) to hit any ball into one of six chalk circles which make up the pool table. (Use the service boxes as pool table outlines.) The ball must stay within the circle in order for the ball to be counted as "in the pocket."

To start, place ten balls in triangular formation in the center of the pool table. Play begins when the first player hits or knocks the balls, using the butt end of a racquet.

Once a ball rests in a pocket, the coach or player immediately removes the ball from the table and sets it aside.

This game can be played with teams or players can participate individually.

The player(s) with the most number of balls "in the pocket" wins the game.

SERVE SURPRISE

Objective: To develop serve direction, control, and consistency.

Focus: Using the hand and forearm to control the face of the racquet when contacting the ball above the level of the head.

Stroke: Serve, groundstroke, volley, lob

Players: 2+

Equipment: Balls, racquets, any objects to be used as targets, paper and pen for messages

Setup and Game: Make up targets with messages hidden underneath them. Players are then asked to hit the targets. Once a target is hit, the message underneath is read. Each message awards a player points, takes away points, or instructs them to do a task to earn points. Make this fun by creating silly things for players to do with a racquet, ball, or a combination in order to earn points.
Examples of possible messages are:
—Lose all points
—The person to the right of you must serve with his/her left hand for 3 turns
—Win the lottery, earn ten points
—Lose a turn
—Earn six points if you can self-rally with a juggle volley
—Volley ten balls in a row

DINOSAUR GAME

Objective: To develop projection skills and improve direction by rolling or hitting balls.

Focus: Using a racquet to hit a ball through a target area.

Stroke: Push groundstroke, groundstroke, or volley from a self-feed

Players: 3+

Equipment: Racquets, balls, target area

Setup and Game: Set up two cones at one end of the court as a target area. Ask one player to be the dinosaur. The dinosaur stands on the other side of the cones by the net. The remainder of the players take on the role of hunters. A bucket of balls should be set up on the center hash marks from each side of the net. In different places around the court other targets can also be set up.

To start the game, ask the first player to roll the ball between the cones using a tennis racquet.

If the ball does not hit the target area, then the dinosaur cage opens up. To get away from the dinosaur, the hunter must move in a clockwise fashion around the court. When the hunter passes the net, a dinosaur is released. The dinosaur tries to tag the hunter by touching him. When a hunter passes a bucket of balls (representing spears) he can pick up one spear(ball) and throw it, or hit it with a racquet, or roll it to a target. If the target is hit, the dinosaur is killed, and a point is earned. If the target is missed by the spear, the hunter must continue running to the other side of the net to pick up another spear and hit a target on that side.

A dinosaur tries to tag the hunter with her hand. After two minutes of playing, the dinosaur automatically becomes extinct. A player has four minutes to get as many points as possible. The winner is the player with the most points.

KNOCK OUT

Objective: To develop direction and height control when hitting balls with a racquet.

Focus: Using a racquet to hit balls over a net by opening the rac-

quet face (vertical racquet face) and changing impact points in front and to the side of the body (horizontal racquet face).

Stroke: Self-fed groundstroke, self-fed volley, serve

Players: 4+

Equipment: Racquets, balls, net

Setup and Game: Line up all the players at the net in an alternating sequence, with a player on one side, the next on the opposite side, etc. All players are facing the net and should have a clear opening to the opponent's field. The coach distributes all balls equally to the players. An equal number of targets are placed on each side of the court. On the signal Go, all players pick up a ball at their feet and hit it toward targets on the other side of the net. The first team to knock down the other teams targets wins. If all balls are hit and no team has yet won, they pick up balls on their side and repeat the process until all of one team's targets are knocked down.

OVER AND UNDER

Objective: To develop height for distance.

Focus: Players open racquet face angles and use different racquet paths in order to create a high loping or low arched ball trajectory. Players attempt to hit balls over or under an outstretched line of string for points.

Stroke: Groundstroke, volley

Players: 4+

Equipment: Racquets, balls, net, two chairs, string four feet or longer

Setup and Game: Place two chairs four feet apart on the court and tie the string to the highest point of each chair. Coaches can assign players to two teams assigning each team the task of hitting the ball over or under the target.

Each time a player successfully hits over or under, the team or individual gains a point. The winner is the team or player with the most points. The coach can feed to students or players can self-feed from a basket.

RAPID FIRE

Objective: To develop directional control when pushing a ball with the racquet.

Focus: Players use the racquet as a hockey stick. They push or strike push the ball to a target area.

Stroke: Pushing skills

Players: 4+

Equipment: Racquet, ball, stopwatch or watch with a second hand

Setup and Game: The coach sets up a line of six balls on the service line that are one-half feet apart. Set up a goal with posts 3 feet apart or more (depending on skill level).

The coach then asks the players to start on the baseline. On the signal Go, the player runs up to the line and hits or pushes the first ball to the goal using their tennis racquets. After each shot the player must run back to the starting line, touch it with the racquet, and then run back for the next shot.

Players have an option and must discover how close to go to release the ball successfully.

Depending on their size and speed, players are given a certain amount of time (say, forty seconds) to shoot their pucks (balls). At the end of the time period no further goals are allowed.

APPLES AND ORANGES

Objective: To develop directional control when pushing a ball using a racquet. To find different color balls and then to push them to specific target areas.

Focus: Using a racquet players will try to push two different colored balls to two matching color target areas.

Stroke: Pushing groundstroke skills

Players: 4+

Equipment: Racquets, two sets of different color balls (red and orange would be best)

Setup and Game: The coach divides players into two teams. On one team are the apple farmers and on the other are the orange farmers. Have the farmers line up along opposite doubles sidelines, one team per sideline. There is one racquet per team. The coach spills and mixes both colored balls in the center court area. On the signal Go, the player closest to the net takes the racquet, finds two of his team's colored tennis balls, and then he pushes them toward the target area (located behind his doubles sideline). After that, the next player takes the racquet and repeats the process. The team that is first to finish farming its crops wins the game. If a team pushes a ball of the wrong color to its area, they lose four points.

HOME RUN KING

Objective: Projection skills for direction and distance.

Focus: Controlling the direction of the ball using a racquet face. Hitting actions, using a swing and racquet path to reach a distant target.

Stroke: Groundstroke, volley, overhead, serve, lob

Players: 2+

Equipment: Racquets, balls, net, fence

Setup and Game: Targets are identified around the court area; they can be areas on the court or objects laid out as markers.

Players perform self-fed strokes and must hit targets consecutively. If two targets are hit, the home run derby starts.

Players are given one chance to hit a ball over the fence surrounding the tennis court for a home run. A home run counts as one run.

The player with the most runs wins. Players collect balls that are hit over the fence after the game is completed.

WATER STAINS

Objective: Projection skills for direction and distance.

Focus: Controlling the direction of the ball using a racquet face.

Hitting actions, using a swing and racquet path to reach a distant target.

Stroke: Serve, overhead, groundstroke, volley (fed)

Players: 4+

Equipment: Racquets, old balls or sponge balls, water

Setup and Game: Take sponge balls, or old tennis balls, and soak them in water. Ask players to hit target areas using the balls.

To score, players count how many times they hit the target area. Each player is given three chances to hit a wet ball into an area.

The winner is the player with the most water stains in the target areas. For a bonus, players can be given a chance to hit a moving target—the coach?

REVOLVING DOOR

Objective: To develop a feel for changing direction when hitting volleys.

Focus: Using a catching action similar to catching a baseball with a glove, with little to no racquet movement. Spinning in a stationary circle, while setting the racquet in the volleying position.

Stroke: Volley, groundstroke

Players: 4+

Equipment: Racquets, balls

Setup and Game: Arrange players close to the net in two lines feeding three balls to each player, one at a time. Players must spin themselves in a stationary circle with their racquet in the volleying position, as if trapped in a revolving door. The revolving door cannot stop to hit the ball; it must continue turning. Players are fed 3 balls each.

With guided discovery, the players should be able to redirect balls into target areas for points.

BUBBLE BASH

Objective: To develop centering skills and hitting at different heights, with some movement.

Focus: Using hands or racquets to hit bubbles. Players move to pop floating bubbles.

Stroke: Volley, overhead, groundstroke action

Players: 2+

Equipment: Racquets, coat hanger, dish, water, liquid dish soap

Setup and Game: Use a coathanger to make a large bubble wand. Make a mixture of two parts water to one part liquid dish soap.

Players are assigned the role of bubble bashers. Their job is to take turns trying to smash bubbles.

Points are awarded for each bubble made after the original bubble is hit (when a bubble is hit other smaller bubbles are created). Coaches or students will count how many bubbles are made after the first hit.

The person with the most points wins.

ANYTHING GOES

Objective: To develop multilateral skills, using hand-eye, foot-eye, head, and chest.

Focus: Using various body parts to keep a ball from rolling on to their side of a net, and trying to send it to the other team's side.

Stroke: Groundstroke, volley, overhead actions without a racquet

Players: 4+

Equipment: Net, balls—preferably a lightweight ball

Setup and Game: Use tennis scoring terminology (15, 30, 40 game). Two teams are created or, if there are few participants, singles can be played.

Players attempt to hit the ball to the other side of the net by using their heads, chests, arms, hands, or other body parts.

One or two players on each side are allowed to use a racquet to hit the ball over the net. The ball can be passed as many times on each team's side. All balls are to be served in an arched path.

The game begins when the first ball is sent over the net.

RECEPTION GAMES

COLOR BLAST

Objective: To develop perception skills, decision making, and ball control when hitting.

Focus: Controlling the racquet face and racquet path at contact in order to master direction, enhance perception, and sharpen decision making.

Stroke: Groundstrokes, volley, overhead

Players: 4+

Equipment: Racquets, balls, net, markers, dye or spray paint

Setup and Game: Participants form two teams. Each team forms a line with a hitter at the front.

A colored blanket is then laid out over half of the court. The other half of the court can be covered with a different color blanket or left uncovered. Tennis balls will then be marked to match the two colors of the court sides.

Each team member is given a chance to hit the tennis balls into the half of the court that matches the balls' color. A point is scored when a player hits a ball into the matching colored court. If a player hits a ball into the wrong court half, he or she loses two points.

The team with the most points wins.

SURPRISE

Objective: To develop perception skills and reaction time using a visual stimulus. To develop speed.

Focus: Fast starting by using an explosive first step away from the player who is "It." Perception and decision making.

Stroke: n.a.

Players: 6+

Equipment: Tennis balls, marker

Setup and Game: Players form a circle in the center of the court, shoulder-width apart. Each player is given a tennis ball, one of which should have a special mark to distinguish it from the others. As balls are handed out, players are instructed not to inspect the ball they are given looking for the mark. At the command "SURPRISE," all players inspect their tennis ball. The player with the specially marked ball tries to tag as many players as he or she can. In the meantime, other players run to a designated safe area. Tagged players sit by the sideline. The players reassemble in a circle once again, and the coach redistributes the balls, making sure to include the marked one.

The last untagged player left on the court wins.

TENNIS TERMINATOR

Objective: To develop side-to-side movement with balance. Reception and projection skills using height and direction.

Focus: Direction is controlled by changing impact in front of and beside the body. Height is controlled by altering the angle of the racquet face relative to the sky.

Stroke: Groundstrokes, volley, serve (with arc), lob

Players: 3+

Equipment: Racquets, balls, tennis court, cones, hoop

Setup and Game: The two service boxes are designated "Space Zones." Use a hoop to represent a planet.

A length of time for play is decided in advance.

Two players (Terminators) are to be positioned on one side while the third player (Defender of the Planet), positions her/himself in the middle of the Space Zones.

The Defender of the Planet tries to save the planet from the attack of the Terminators by volleying balls back from them.

The Terminators try to land a missile (the ball) on the planet surface (inside the hoop) using self-fed volleys and groundstrokes.

The Defender who stops the most missiles wins the game.

SCRAMBLED EGGS

Objective: To set up early behind incoming tennis balls.

Focus: Develop footwork by moving behind balls being received, using quick explosive steps.

Stroke: Groundstroke, volley, overhead

Players: 2+

Equipment: Balls, net

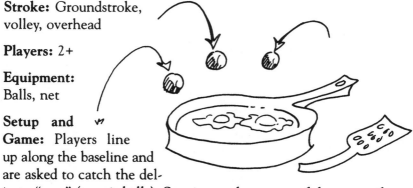

Setup and Game: Players line up along the baseline and are asked to catch the delicate "eggs" (tennis balls). Starting at the center of the court, the coach feeds four balls to each player in a random manner. Players will earn one point for each "egg" caught. The player who catches a dozen eggs wins.

The players must catch the balls in their hands or, to make the game more challenging, with the help of their racquet.

To decrease the level of difficulty, balls (eggs) can be caught after one bounce.

STOP SIGN

Objective: To help develop a ready position prior to hitting strokes.

Focus: Players must stop their forward momentum by using a split step, in which the feet are in line with each other and facing the net. If a player takes a step after the coach touches the ball, he must take three steps backward.

Stroke: Groundstroke, volley, overhead

Players: 2+

Equipment: Balls

Setup and Game: Players line up as far off the baseline as possible but still facing the net (by the fence). The coach stands on the other side of the net. When the coach tosses the ball in the air, all players can run toward the net. But when he makes an action to hit the ball, all players must stop dead in their tracks using the split step, taking ready position. The racquet must also be in front, and its head must be toward the sky in traditional ready position stance. If a player moves after the coach has contacted the ball and is spotted by the coach, then that player must begin again at the fence. The winner is the first player to reach the net and touch it.

GOALIE

Objective: To develop lateral movement when receiving various types of balls.

Focus: Kids will use their feet to stop balls from going into the goal area.

Stroke: Footwork development for use with all strokes

Players: 2+

Equipment: Racquets, balls, net area

Setup and Game: The coach is the shooter, and the kids take turns being the goalie. Each goalie faces three shots. The winning goalie is the player with the least amount of goals allowed, after all the balls are used.

OH, MY ACHING HEAD

Objective: To develop body awareness and concentration.

Focus: To use the hand and forearm to steady the racquet in order to center the ball in the middle of the strings.

Stroke: Centering skills, self-ground stroke, self-volley, ground-stroke and volley from a feed, serving, overhead

Players: 6+

Equipment: Racquets, balls, net, basket

Setup and Game: Each of two teams takes turns slowly spinning each individual from the opposing team. The person being spun should have her eyes closed (this is the person with a "headache"), while a ball is placed on her racquet. The person with a headache then walks toward a target area with her eyes open, dropping the ball into a basket, or hitting the ball toward a certain area or target over the net. The object of the game is to be the first team to drop the most balls into the basket, or hit the most balls over the net.

BINGO

Objective: Receiving balls from different directions and different heights. Perception and recognition skills.

Focus: Using hands or racquets to catch and center balls on the string bed.

Stroke: Groundstroke, volley

Players: 4+

Equipment: Racquets, balls, markers, paper, small rocks

Setup and Game: Mark tennis balls with different colored permanent markers and make bingo cards using those same colors.

Players are told to catch the different colored balls fed to them either on their string beds or hands. Corresponding squares on their bingo cards are marked using a small stone or other marker.

The first player to fill her or his bingo card wins.

KABOOM!

Objective: To develop perception and reception skills with minor projection skills.

Focus: Players focus on recognizing safe and dangerous "X" balls, which are clearly marked to differentiate them from the rest. Students work on opening the string bed in order to promote an arched trajectory, and on making decisions and getting set behind the ball.

Stroke: Groundstroke, volley, overhead

Players: 4+

Equipment: Racquets, balls, 1–3 specially marked balls

Setup and Game: Two lines next to each other, are made single file facing the net. Balls will be fed to the players. Some of the balls are safe to hit. Others are marked "X." These are the bombs. Bombs should not be hit.

The first two players may decide to hit the ball fed to them by the coach over the net. If the player is able to hit the ball fed to her over the net, then she is awarded a point. If the dangerous "X" bomb is fed and hit by the player, he is automatically out of the game. The winner is the player with the most points or the last person out.

STOP THE AVALANCHE

Objective: To be able to develop reception skills for balls coming from different directions.

Focus: Using hands or racquets, players attempt to stop balls from reaching the target line.

Stroke: Centering skills

Players: 4+

Equipment: Racquets and balls

Setup and Game: Divide the players into two snowplow teams. Each team will take turns attempting to stop an avalanche from crashing down on the town (passing a designated line). The coach

feeds a specific number of balls (snowballs) from one area. The coach may roll, bounce, or loft the ball into the designated area, depending on the skill being developed. The coach will then count how many balls got through.

The next snowplows take their turn, and the team allowing the least amount of snow (balls) through wins.

CRAZY FOOT TAG

Objective: Develop various footwork movements to be used in a game of tag.

Focus: Moving with crosssteps, shuffle, carioca, wide steps, small steps, tippy-toe steps, heel steps, etc. Centering a ball in the middle of the string bed of the racquet while moving.

Stroke: Centering skills, self-rally volley, self-rally groundstroke

Players: 6+

Equipment: Racquets, balls, players' shoes

Setup and Game: Scatter players over the court with one player designated as It. The object is to tag the free players with the non-racquet hand while the other hand is centering a ball in the middle of the strings. The difficult part is that the coach will, throughout the game, call out (every 2 to 3 minutes) the type of steps that the players must use. If a player is not doing the footwork, he receives a warning. If he continues with the wrong footwork, he is automatically called It.

Once a player is tagged she also becomes It, and she also chases the free players. If while chasing the free players a person who is free loses the ball off the string bed, then he must retrieve it and then stand still for five seconds, counting the seconds out loud. The winner is the last player to remain untagged.

PEPPER

Objective: To develop reaction speed, and hand-eye coordination when volleying.

Focus: Adjusting the racquet in the hand in order to be prepared early to contact a ball. The earlier a player sets his racquet, the better the control.

Stroke: Volley

Players: 4+

Equipment: Racquets, balls

Setup and Game: The coach gathers four players and places them in a semicircle positioning himself in the center of the four players.

The coach hits the ball to each player. The player immediately bounces the ball back to the coach, using her hands or racquet.

The winner is the player who hits the most balls back to the coach within a set time.

BODYBUILDER

Objective: To develop balance when hitting and receiving balls.

Focus: Controlling balance by holding the body still like a statue after hitting a ball.

Stroke: Groundstroke, volley, serve, overhead

Players: 3+

Equipment: Racquets, balls, net

Setup and Game: Participants form split lines. The coach feeds balls to the left and right of each player, with some balls being fed short and some deep. Immediately after hitting a ball, the player must pose like a bodybuilder for three seconds before hitting the next ball.

THIS THEN THAT

Objective: To develop various kinds of coordination using a racquet to work on reception and sending skills.

Focus: Getting familiar with the racquet, including the grips, by manipulating it in relation to the body.

Stroke: Various

Players: 1+

Equipment: Racquets, balls, net

Setup and Game: Players are fed balls while in a line and must perform an action prior to hitting the ball. The coach will challenge each player to perform a specific action such as turning around, sitting down, spinning the racquet around the waist, neck, or ankles, and then to immediately hit the ball.

RUN FOR YOUR LIFE TENNIS

Objective: To develop running skills and the ability to change direction when holding a racquet.

Focus: Players run to balls hit all over the court by the coach and attempt to touch the balls before they bounce two times. Players will mimic a running action as if they did not have a racquet in hand. The pumping of the arms when running should be encouraged.

Stroke: n.a.

Players: 2+

Equipment: Racquets, balls

Setup and Game: Players take turns trying to touch balls using a racquet before the balls bounce twice. Note that only one player at a time runs for the balls. The coach will ask players to start at the net and then she will feed them over their heads, left, right, short, and deep. The player who can touch six out of six balls gets a point. Safety is important, so make sure that there is one child assigned to clearing balls off the court during the chase. The winner is the one with the most points.

PICK A POCKET

Objective: To develop awareness of the racquet by centering the ball in different sections of a special racquet head.

Focus: Reception skills, primarily changing centering locations on a racquet.

Stroke: Groundstroke, volley, overhead, serve

Players: 6+

Equipment: Coat hangers, plastic bags, two racquets, tennis balls, tape (to attach plastic bags to hangers and hangers to racquets)

Setup and Game: Attach plastic bags to four coat hangers so that they form pockets. Each pocket is then attached to the tennis racquet so that four pockets are evenly spaced out around the racquet. Two such racquets should be made.

Players are then asked to take turns catching balls in the pockets. Teams line up on one side of the net. One by one, team members throw a tennis ball over the net at the catcher on the other side.

Once a ball is caught in a pocket, the catcher takes the place of the last person in line. The last person in line then becomes the next catcher.

The game continues until all team members have had a chance to catch a ball.

GOOFY GROUNDBALLS

Objective: To develop skills when receiving balls from different directions and heights, using hands or racquets.

Focus: To enhance depth perception skills by coordinating footwork according to the bounce of the ball.

Stroke: Groundstrokes, overhead

Players: 3+

Equipment: Racquets, balls

Setup and Game: Players form two lines. The coach then feeds balls to each player, and they attempt to catch them after a specified number of bounces determined by the coach. Players can catch the ball using their hands or the racquet face. The command might therefore be: "Catch the ball in three bounces."

A point is awarded each time a player catches a ball after the correct number of bounces. The first player to earn eight points wins.

BODY PARTS

Objective: The development of body awareness.

Focus: Discovery of balance when the body is under constraints.

Stroke: Various

Players: 2+

Equipment: Racquets, balls, net

Setup and Game: Any rally-type game or target game but this time an error causes the loss of the use of a body part, such as a hand or a foot, and the player must then alter play in order to compensate for the "loss."

FIRE FIRE FIRE!

Objective: To develop reception (centering) skills in a team situation.

Focus: Using hand-eye coordination to catch balls using an empty ball container.

Stroke: n.a.

Players: 8+

Equipment: Two empty tennis ball tubes

Setup and Game: There is a blazing fire; a house is burning. Call the firefighters quickly.

The coach divides the players into teams. Teams line up in single file two feet from the net. The coach stands with a bucket of balls on the other side of the net, on the service line, and he continuously alternates feeding tennis balls (they represent waterballs) to the firefighters. The first fire-fighter from each team should be given an empty hose (ball tube). Her job is to fill it with water by catching one waterball at a time using the empty hose to catch with. The firefighter should catch the waterballs in the air or on a bounce, after which she must immediately pass the hose to the next person in line. The process is repeated until the hose is filled. At that time the team is awarded one point.

The balls in the tube are taken by the last firefighter and emptied into a container. The next firefighter in line starts catching again.

The team with the most waterballs collected in the container wins.

BUBBLE COMPASS

Objective: To discover the effects of the environment, in this case wind, on the trajectory and direction of a bubble. Visualization and anticipation are also practiced.

Focus: Wind can have a critical effect on the way a ball travels or is received. Players will anticipate where the bubbles will travel by the direction of the wind.

Stroke: Volley, groundstroke (safety, distance, the players), overhead

Players: 4+

Equipment: Racquets (optional), hanger (for bubble maker), dish-soap and water mixture (two parts water to one part liquid dish soap)

Setup and Game: The coach positions himself in the middle of the court and asks the players to stand where they think the bubble will travel. When all the players have chosen their position, the coach begins to blow bubbles.

The players attempt to catch the bubbles in their hands or by using their racquets. They should anticipate where they think the bubbles might land.

The player who touches the most bubbles wins. Players can use racquets to perform stroke actions.

HELICOPTER

Objective: To develop balance and coordinated movement (future advanced movement work for slice approach, advanced volley)

Focus: To develop crossover footwork using the carioca footwork step used in creating proper spacing from the ball for impact.

Stroke: Centering skill, self-rally volley, self-rally groundstroke

Players: 4+

Equipment: Tennis balls, racquets optional

Setup and Game: All the players as helicopters line up on a starting line, and when the

---

coach says "Go," all the helicopters take off and race around the court. Copters can only move with carioca-type footwork. If the footwork is not carioca then the copter is taken out of the air and put in the shop.

To do the carioca footwork, the arms are outstretched at chest height and sway left and right (staying at chest height) like helicopter rotor blades, and the left leg crossed behind the right. Then on the next stride (moving to the right), the left leg passes in front, then back again. At the end of each lap each helicopter must fill up with gas to continue flying laps.

Gas is taken by catching a tennis ball tossed by the coach(es). The winner is the copter with the most laps.

ROTTEN APPLES

Objective: To develop perception and decision making with some projection skills using any stroke except the serve.

Focus: Players attempt to hit "safe" balls over the net while avoiding different colored or marked balls, using hitting actions.

Stroke: Groundstroke, volley, overhead

Players: 2+

Equipment: Racquets, balls, net, six marked balls

Setup and Game: Players try to hit as many balls as they can into a target area or over the net. The coach will feed balls in very short intervals (not fast/hard). Either the first person to hit ten balls over the net or the one to hit the most safe balls wins. Balls that are marked or colored are the rotten apples. Points are not awarded if any of these balls are hit.

WARRIORS

Objective: To develop reception skills of blocking and catching when volleying.

Focus: Players use a racquet as a shield to block and deflect balls away from themselves.

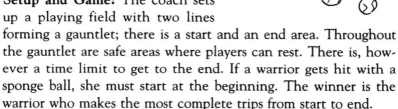

Stroke: Volley, overhead blocking action

Players: 2+

Equipment: Racquets, sponge balls, grassy area

Setup and Game: The coach sets up a playing field with two lines forming a gauntlet; there is a start and an end area. Throughout the gauntlet are safe areas where players can rest. There is, however a time limit to get to the end. If a warrior gets hit with a sponge ball, she must start at the beginning. The winner is the warrior who makes the most complete trips from start to end.

TIMBER!

Objective: To develop anticipation skills.

Focus: By asking leading questions about everyday occurrences kids will learn what anticipation is. For example: "What color comes after green with a stoplight; or if an ice cube is left on the tennis court, what happens." Create some tennis related questions such as, "If a person looks like he's completely off balance, can he hit the ball over the net with control?"

Stroke: Pushing skills

Players: 4+

Equipment: Racquets, balls

Setup and Game: Ask players to line up their racquets on edge with the butt facing down on the ground. Then ask the players to answer questions, or to do some self-rally tasks. The player with the correct answer or completion of the task gets a shot at hitting a ball or rolling a ball toward the first racquet trying to knock them all down.

BANANA SPLIT STEPS

Objective: To develop split steps, which will contribute to good movement skills laterally, left, right, forward, and backward.

Focus: Walking forward with a short hop to an immediate stance with feet a shoulder-width apart and the knees slightly bent.

Stroke: n.a.

Players: 4+

Equipment: Racquet, balls

Setup and Game: Have the players take turns going forward and then they must move on the Coach's verbal cue, calling left, right, forward, backward, or with visual cues using the hand to point to the direction where the player is to move.

To gain half points, a player has to split step at a designated mark on the ground. Simultaneously, the coach is to call out or show a direction to which the player will break, after which a ball is tossed to the area. The player must then catch the ball after the bounce, in the air, or by letting it touch the racquet to gain a full point.

A point is awarded for every successful split step and catch. The winner is the player with the most points earned.

GORILLA STEPS

Objective: To develop a low center of gravity, which will enhance good movement skills when changes of direction are made.

Focus: Low arm movements with knees bent.

Stroke: n.a.

Players: 4+

Equipment: Balls

Setup and Game: Players are asked to act like gorillas and to make gorilla sounds. To act like a gorilla they should swing their arms. Coaches may want to feed balls at different heights to the players asking them to catch the balls only at a certain height using their hands.

HUMAN SHIELD

Objective: Develop higher-level centering skills with partial hitting actions, future serve, and overhead work.

Focus: Use racquets or hands to stop balls traveling above the head.

Stroke: Overhead, serve, high volley

Players: 2+

Equipment: Racquets, balls

Setup and Game: Players will pretend they are radar detectors, trying to destroy missiles. The coach feeds balls to players over their heads, one by one, and the players must stop the missiles by blocking them with their racquets. A point is scored each time a missile is kept from landing on a specific area.

STUFF IT

Objective: To develop teamwork and hand-eye coordination using the entire body as a moving human closet.

Focus: Using the hands, arms, forearms, ankles, legs, and neck.

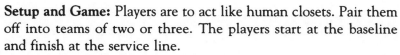

Stroke: n.a.

Players: 2+

Equipment: Balls

Setup and Game: Players are to act like human closets. Pair them off into teams of two or three. The players start at the baseline and finish at the service line.

Each team will have one designated stuffer and one or two human closets. On the signal Go, the stuffer places balls on their partner who must walk to the finish line. Any balls that have not fallen on the ground after passing the finish line are collected by each team and counted as points. Any balls that have fallen do not count as points.

After the human closet has passed the end line, he returns for a refilling of balls. There is a time limit of two minutes, after which the balls are counted.

The team with the most balls collected wins.

TENNIS ATHLETE'S FOOT

Objective: To develop footwork balance and coordination.

Focus: Using the toe, top, or side of the foot to hit balls before they bounce twice.

Stroke: n.a.

Players: 6+

Equipment: Balls

Setup and Game: Ask one player to come to the center of the court, while the other players wait their turn. The coach then feeds balls at a slow interval, and the player must move to the ball. Before the ball bounces twice, the player must hit, or tap the ball with her foot to score a point.

If the player can hit the ball over the net with her foot, then the player gets five points. A special bonus is given if a player can hit three over the net with her foot. The player who does this, automatically wins the game.

SHADOW TENNIS

Objective: To develop observation skills and improve reaction time.

Focus: Students use their eyes to track the shadow of a tennis ball until the ball arrives in their outstretched hands. Shuffling movement may be needed to place oneself behind the ball.

Stroke: n.a.

Players: 2+

Equipment: Racquets, balls, shining sun

Setup and Game: Players try to catch balls rolled to them by a coach by following the shadow of the ball until it arrives in their hand or hits the racquet. Players take turns attempting to catch balls in their hands. They are not allowed to look at the coach, or watch for the release of the ball. Rather, they are to look almost completely down. Points are awarded for successful catches. It is very important that the coach roll balls where the sun can cast a shadow. The coach will observe the players' eyes and judge if they are looking at the ball or shadow.

RALLY GAMES

SHARK!

Objective: To develop rallying skills when changing the height of balls being sent and received.

Focus: Depending on the ball control specified, the racquet face is opened or closed to receive balls at different heights by moving up or back in the court.

Stroke: Groundstrokes, volley, lobs

Players: 4+

Equipment: Racquets, balls, net

Setup and Game: Players rally over the net as partners. Ten balls must be rallied in a row for a point to be scored. As the ball is rallied, players count the number of rallies out loud.

In the meantime, one player takes on the role of "shark." The shark's role is to eat balls that fly too low to the net. As such, he/she blocks balls either by standing on a chair or by using a racquet. The shark can swim, or leap from the water only along the line of the net. Partners with the most points win.

MINI TENNIS DOUBLES

Objective: Developing rallying with partners in a competitive situation.

Focus: Using reception and projection skills when rallying with partners. Reception (get set behind the ball), projection (open racquet face).

Stroke: Groundstroke, volley

Players: 4+

Equipment: Racquets, balls, tennis court

Setup and Game: This is a mini-court version of doubles with simple underhand serving. There is no driving or smashing allowed. All balls must be hit in an arched trajectory, including volleys. Players will take turns serving crosscourt underhand, four times each, then switch.

Points are won each time a team player performs an error or hits an unreturnable ball.

AROUND THE WORLD—VARIATION

Objective: To develop rally skills and enhance projection and reception skills.

Focus: Movement, footwork to get set up behind the ball like a goalie. Reception, setting the racquet on the forehand / backhand side before the ball bounces on the player's side. Projection, using an open racquet face and a little low to high racquet path.

Stroke: Groundstroke

Players: 7+

Equipment: Racquets, balls, net

Setup and Game: In this game, the players must see who can be the most consistent in hitting the ball over the net. ·

The total number of players are divided on either side of the net so that there are two lines formed. Each line starts on the baseline in the center of the court. On the signal Go, the first player hits the ball over the net with a forehand, and then she runs to the other side of the net and joins the end of the other line. Meanwhile, the ball that was struck is to be hit by the first player on the other side of the net. After the first player hits, he also runs to the other line and joins it.

The ball continues to be rallied until a mistake is made. The player who makes the mistake is out, or loses one life (two lives and he is out of the game and must sit out). The winner is the last person on the court who has not made the maximum number of mistakes. Players are allowed to let the ball bounce once or twice, depending on the skill level of the children.

BEAT THE COACH

Objective: Height and directional control, and basic tactics.

Focus: Direction controlled by changing the impact in front of and beside the body, and the face of the racquet at impact, height over the net controlled by tilting the racquet face toward the sky so there is a change in the angle of the vertical racquet face.

Stroke: Groundstroke, volley, overhead lob, serve

Players: 2+

Equipment: Racquets, balls, tennis court

Setup and Game: Have paired teams play points two on one, against the coach. Students are asked to hit balls into the open courts away from the coach—who should position himself on alternate sides of the court so as to create a large opening for players to hit to.

The coach must play the entire court, including the doubles boundaries, while the two players cover only the singles court service boxes. The object of the game is to beat the coach.

T.E.N.N.I.S.

Objective: To build consistency by sending and receiving balls.

Focus: Using the racquet to hit balls in an arched trajectory, reception and projection skills

Stroke: Groundstroke, volley

Players: 2+

Equipment: Racquet, balls

Setup and Game: Players are paired off and are asked to rally a certain number of balls in a row. When a set number is reached, the pair receives a letter *T*, then *E* etc., until T-E-N-N-I-S is spelled.

To vary the game, players can rally over an obstacle.

SPACE TENNIS

Objective: To develop striking skills using the hands above the head. Development of motor skills above the head.

Focus: Each player must attempt to keep the ball in the air by hitting it with either the racquet or the hand. Players will either sit, or stand in place, or hop on one foot to make it seem less like traditional tennis.

This game will help develop a higher level of actions and motor skills.

Stroke: Volley, overhead, serve

Players: 4+

Equipment: Racquets, net, beach balls or balloons

Setup and Game: The coach divides the players into two teams and then asks the players to stand on opposite sides of the net on the court. Players pretend to play tennis while remaining in their space using a balloon as a ball. Scoring will be the same as tennis scoring so the coach might want to introduce the scoring system at this time. If the kids are too young, then he could use total points.

BLIND SPACE TENNIS

Objective: This game will help develop a higher level of actions and motor skills.

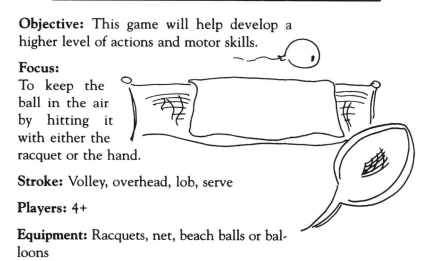

Focus:
To keep the ball in the air by hitting it with either the racquet or the hand.

Stroke: Volley, overhead, lob, serve

Players: 4+

Equipment: Racquets, net, beach balls or balloons

Setup and Game: Place a towel or a blanket over the net in order to prevent the players from seeing the balloon until it is over the net. All players sit down with legs crossed, and they play tennis in this position using the balloon as a ball.

Tennis scoring (15, 30, 40, etc.) can be used, or, if very young children are playing, highest total points wins.

DESERT TENNIS

Objective: To understand court geometry while developing rally skills.

Focus: To discover movement patterns front and back, left and right. To discover passing and receiving skills. To demystify the court and its angles when playing the entire court surface.

Stroke: Groundstroke, volley, lob, overhead with arc, serve

Players: 8+

Equipment: Racquets, net, balls

Setup and Game: Form two teams. Teams spread themselves over the court, and surrounding boundaries. One team should be on each side of the net. Players are allowed to play balls no matter how many bounces. The ball is dead and the point is awarded to the other team when a player makes a shot into the net, or if the ball rolls on the ground. Players can choose either to pass the ball to a teammate or hit immediately over the net. The ball can be hit around or over the net. The winning team is the team with the most points or the first to reach a specified number.

"36"

Objective: To develop consistency and basic tactics.

Focus: Consistency by setting up early with body sideways and racquet back using open racquet face (vertical racquet angle) and small swing length action.

Stroke: Groundstroke, volley

Players: 4+

Equipment: Racquets, balls, net

Setup and Game: Players will rally four balls in a row over the net and then play out the point. The designated top of the court will play each point. He must obtain six points before the opponents reach three points.

If the person at the top of the court reaches six points, then he erases all existing points, at which time the group starts again at zero.

The two are to alternate playing points against the one. Basically, the leader must double the points earned by the others to win.

DOUBLES ALLEY RALLY

Objective: To outrally an opponent, using an arc trajectory.

Focus: To develop an understanding of impact point. To discover the effects of a horizontal racquet-face angle (impact points in front or beside the body) and a vertical racquet-face angle (opening and closing the face of the racquet).

Stroke: Groundstroke, volley

Players: 4+

Equipment: Racquet, balls, net

Setup and Game: Players stand beside the doubles alley and are designated numbers 1–4. Player one plays against player two, player three against player four. Winners play winners and second place plays second place.

Players feed each other a ball at waist height and play out the point using the doubles alley as the court boundaries.

MINI TENNIS ANGLES

Objective: To practice creating angles using less arc and ball speed.

Focus: To learn the use of racquet angles and small racquet lengths (actual distance the racquet travels) in order to control racquet speed.

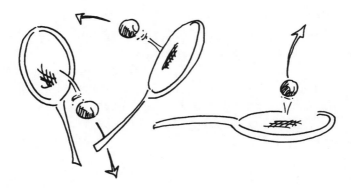

Stroke: Groundstroke

Players: 4+

Equipment: Racquet, balls, net

Setup and Game: Players use the service boxes and the net as mini tennis courts. Each player is numbered 1–4. Player one plays player two in the add boxes, and simultaneously, player three plays player four in the deuce boxes. The players try to move the ball in the box and attempt to create angles using less arc or ball speed.

HOT TAMALE

Objective: To develop reaction time and hand-eye coordination.

Focus: Tapping the ball upward in a continuous rally using the hand and forearm, no racquets are used.

Stroke: n.a.

Players: 4+

Equipment: Balls

Setup and Game: Position players one foot from the net facing the coach. The coach can stand on the same side of net for lower-skilled players and on the other side for more advanced players. A maximum of four players at one time play against the coach. Balls are hit back to the coach using the palm of the hand. If a player hits the ball into the net, a new player takes his place in line. The winner is the player who can hit ten balls back to the coach first.

MISCELLANEOUS GAMES

ARE YOU A FAMOUS TENNIS PLAYER YET?

Objective: A good way for kids to meet one another.

Focus: Giving kids a task that gives them a reason for introducing themselves to each other.

Stroke: n.a.

Players: 6+

Equipment: One piece of paper and one pencil for each child

Setup and Game: On the first day of tennis camp, all kids should meet each other. This game breaks the ice smoothly and effectively. Give each child a pencil and a paper listing all the kids participating in the lessons for the day or week. The task is to get them to ask each other for autographs by saying, "Are you a famous tennis player?" Each child answers yes and signs where his or her name is. After each child has a signature beside each name on his or her list, the game is over for that child.

TENNIS LADDERS AND SLIDES

Objective: To develop different self-rally skills, projection skills, and reception skills.

Focus: Using various body segments relative to objectives selected, such as hand, forearm, shoulder.

Stroke: Self-rally groundstroke, self-rally volley

Players: 6+

Equipment: Racquets, balls, paper (for instructions), and towels (to represent slides or ladders)

Setup and Game: The court is set up as a board game. Squares are marked off with different tasks attached to each. Players pretend to be playing pieces. Participants roll the dice to move to differ-ent spaces on the "board."

To earn a chance to roll the dice, players must perform a task. If while moving along the board, a player lands on a marked square that has a ladder or slide on it she or he moves accordingly.

A finish line is marked off on the board. The first player to reach the finish line wins.

Ideas for Play:
1. Catch a ball fed by the coach, and you move two spaces ahead.
2. Bounce the ball fifteen times while standing on one foot, and you move ahead three spaces.
3. Rally with the coach ten times in a row, and move four spaces ahead. Miss, and move back one space.

FINISH LINE

Objective: A fun way of structuring tasks in a station-by-station format.

Focus: The coach designates the focus points to be used relative to the tasks created.

Stroke: n.a.

Players: 8+

Equipment: Racquets, balls, net (optional)

Setup and Game: The coach chooses six places on the tennis court where tasks are to be performed. At each sta-tion there will be a number of balls and a simple explanation of the task to be done. The children are lined up in single file. The first person gets to attempt the first task. If she is successful, then she continues on to the next task. If the first person fails, then she stays at the task station waiting until all the players in the line have had a chance to perform the first task. Only then can she attempt the task again. As player after player succeeds and fails, children become stranded at different task stations. The winner is the first person to the end.

SPELLING SPOOKS

Objective: To support children's use of correct tennis terms.

Focus: Children will spell words associated with tennis.

Stroke: n.a.

Players: 4+

Equipment: Tennis balls, paper, pens

Setup and Game: The coach stands in the middle of a large circle of kids. She announces loudly a word related to tennis, and each player takes a turn attempting to spell the word before the ball bounces a certain number of times. If the child spells the word correctly, he receives a point. The winner is the child with the most points.

CHARADES TENNIS

Objective: Getting to know a racquet, ball, and the tennis court through acting out everyday events.

Focus: Players are encouraged to use the racquet, balls, or court to role play.

Stroke: n.a.

Players: 4+

Equipment:
Racquets, balls, slips
of paper, pens

Setup and Game: Prior to playing
the game, a number of scenarios to
act out, or objects to describe, are
written down on individual slips of
paper. Divide the players into two teams.
This will promote their getting to know
each other. Each team member is given a chance to enact a scenario or describe an object to his team members. Points are awarded for each charade guessed by the team members.

The team with the most points wins.

JUGGLER'S JAMBOREE

Objective: To develop hand-eye coordination.

Focus: Students will perform various tasks using tennis balls, by themselves or with a partner.

Stroke: n.a.

Players: 4+

Equipment: Tennis balls

Setup and Game: All tasks
are explained by the coach
or whoever is leading the
game. All skills can be performed individually, in pairs, or in small groups. The coach can challenge participants by asking who will be the fastest individual, pair, or group to perform the task, pairing off kids in twos. Give each pair two balls, have them face each other, a foot apart, and then place a ball in the left hand of

both players. On the signal Go, have each player pass the ball to the right hand of his partner. Then have each player quickly pass the ball just received to her own left hand. Each player again repeats the exchange. See how many times players can pass a ball to his partner in one minute. A variation could be to start the ball in each player's right hand and reverse the direction of the ball path.

JOKE OF THE DAY

Objective: A relaxation task for fun during a rest or break.

Focus: Socialization outside of tennis play.

Stroke: n.a.

Players: 2+

Equipment: Imagination, joke book optional

Setup and Game: While players are taking a break from their tennis workout, ask them to plan a skit with a partner, or to imitate somebody in the group for points, or simply tell the funniest joke they know (censorship may be advisable).

TENNIS BALL SPUD

Objective: Reaction time and movement, and auditory perception.

Focus: Reacting to an auditory cue (a word) and then moving. Using the racquet or hands to catch a ball, then throwing the ball at a person below the waist.

Stroke: n.a.

Players: 4+

Equipment: Sponge ball or a soft type of ball

Setup and Game: All players are positioned in a circle. The coach whispers a number to each player after which time he tosses the ball up in the middle of the circle. With the toss of the ball, the coach calls out a number. The player whose number is called attempts to catch the ball with hands or racquet, as the others run away. When the child whose number is called catches the

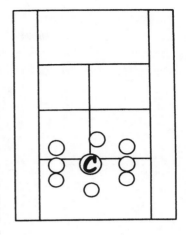

ball, the players stop, and the child then throws the ball below the waist at any of the other players.

A player who is hit is out and sits on the sideline. The kids are placed in a circle once again, and the process is repeated. When there are two kids left, the player whose number is called must hit the other player or she loses.

STROKES

Objective: To create different skills by using a variety of strokes in one game.

Focus: Players are fed balls and asked to hit a particular stroke by the coach such as forehand, backhand, volley, groundstroke, serve to an area, or over the net.

Stroke: Various strokes

Players: 4+

Equipment: Racquets, balls, net

Setup and Game: Kids form one or two lines or (depending on the number of players involved). The coach or group leader announces the stroke to be hit and then feeds the player or asks the player to serve. If the player does not complete the stroke, they are out. Players can have one or two chances before they are declared out.

SHADOW DANCING

Objective: Speed of reaction and foot-eye coordination.

Focus: Visual cues and subsequent reactions using a players' feet to avoid one another. By watching the shadow of the partner, a player can mimic the actions of the player.

Stroke: n.a.

Players: 2+

Equipment: A shining sun

Setup and Game: Basically, the game is played by having one person chase the other's shadow by imitating whatever that person's shadow does.

If at any time, the shadow is not touching the chaser the other player gets a point. Be sure the area is safe for each team.

WRONG WAY IS THE RIGHT WAY

Objective: To build skills with the nondominant hand.

Focus: Using the nondominant hand to throw, catch, or hit tennis balls.

Stroke: n.a.

Players: 2+

Equipment: Balls, racquets

Setup and Game: The coach asks all players to use the non-dominant or weaker hand. If the player does not know which is her right or wrong hand, she should be asked to throw a ball. The hand used to throw with would be the dominant hand.

Players line up on one side of the net to do tasks such as self-rallying, centering the ball, or hitting over the net. Players earn points for completing tasks. Tasks should proceed from simple to complex.

The object of the game is to accumulate as many points as possible.

TENNIS POKER

Objective: To create a fun visual way of keeping track of scoring.

Focus: Using cards to enhance a game

Stroke: n.a.

Players: 2+

Equipment: Deck of cards

Setup and Game: Using ordinary playing cards as points, the coach determines which values the cards will be given. Any type of card game can be played.

Each time a player earns a point or wins a game he is given a card. This is a way to make the game more enjoyable.

FORTUNE-TELLER

Objective: To develop various projection and reception skills. To develop creativity and independence by having each child create a task.

Focus: Students will create tasks using centering skills, self-hitting from a drop-fed ball to a specific target or area. Movement can be used as an option.

Stroke: Various skills chosen by players

Players: 4+

Equipment: Racquets, balls, net

Setup and Game: The coach lines up the players and lets the first fortuneteller tell his own fortune. The fortuneteller creates a task that he think he can perform. If he performs the task successfully, then all the other players must attempt to perform the same one, and he tells another fortune. If a player is unable to perform the task, then she will receive a letter which spells the word _____ (make up a funny word).

If the first fortuneteller can't perform the task he created, then the next person becomes the fortuneteller and this player creates her own task.

The winner is the person who has the least number of letters.

Examples of possible tasks:
—Self-drop feed and hit the service box
—Self-drop feed and hit ball to the doubles alley
—Hitting with the nondominant hand
—Hit over the fence

Acknowledgments

Mom and Dad, once again thanks for everything in my life. I hope that one day I may be able to raise my kids as successfully as you did.

Laura Ozolins, any United States university would be proud to have you as part of their tennis squad. You are a high-performance player with an exceptional work ethic. I am sure you can achieve any goal you set your heart and mind on.

Thanks to Stan Smith for his encouragement, support, advice, and most important, his acceptance. He is a big reason that this book exists today. Words like *champion, grace, class, competitive spirit, work ethic, determination,* and *perseverance* come to mind when I think of you. All that is rare to find in one person.

My sister Vivian, the epitome of hard work and dedication, who always goes out of her way to help the family and me.

My sister Vickie, artist extraordinaire; *great illustrations,* Sis. Thanks again for your help with the book; you gave me great insight and direction.

My brother Victor, whose entrepreneurial ideas are incredible, for putting up with my stubborn side and tolerating my "big words."

My grandmother Lola Ma, thanks, Lolls, for never, ever complaining to a seven-year-old about bringing home friends for lunch, and thanks for always pretending to love my dinosaur and space adventure drawings.

My little Willow, for "giving" to me unconditionally and for showing me how to love life even more. Thanks for sharing your ideas, compromising when you didn't have to, and for listening to me when I needed someone to talk to.

Ken, I can't believe that ever since kindergarten we're still best friends.

Andy, for your help with the book, your generosity, and your never ending wit. I'm glad that you're part of the family.

Arthur Ashe, a man who was bigger than the game, a champion who took responsibility to help others advance in life. His legacy lives on in the game and in our communities.

Tim Gullikson, the man who gave all he had to the game and the people around him. A role model without equal.

All the coaches and superstars who supported the book: Stan Smith, Tom Gullikson, Nick Bollettieri, Dennis Van der Meer, John Lloyd, Pete Sampras, André Agassi, Rod Laver, Virginia Wade, Luke and Murphy Jensen, Cliff Drysdale, Peter Burwash, Carling Bassett, Malivai Washington, Gigi Fernandez and friends, Martina Hingis, Pam Shriver, Dick Gould, Dr. Jim Loehr, Dr. Jack Groppel, Todd Martin, Wayne Ferreira, Grant Connell, Louis Cayer, Dr. Don Chu, David Higdon, Peter Bodo, and all the agents of I.M.G., Proserv, Advantage, and other management companies.

All the tennis federations, organizations, programs, and people who introduce children to our sport: the U.S.T.A., A.T.P.'s Smash tennis, T.I.A. grassroots initiatives, Nike Play programs, the Play Tennis America program, Play Tennis Canada, U.S.P.T.A.'s Tennis Across America, Little Starter Tennis Program, and all inner city tennis programs around the world. Keep up the great work!!!

All those coaches who have sacrificed and gone out of their way to ensure opportunity and growth in their students.

Parents, the often unsung heroes of tennis and sport.

Coach Extraordinaire Louis Cayer, who I loved working with for many years. He showed me that there is no finish line in coaching and that all coaches need to improve themselves no matter what their reputation, position or status.

For sound advice and opportunities: Ron Woods (U.S.T.A.)

Dave Miley (I.T.F.), Wendy Pattenden, and Robert Bettauer (Tennis Canada), Pierre LaMarche.

The Tennis Canada staff: Bob, Derek, Carmel, Jane, Loretto, Stacy, Chang-er, Peter, Colette, Vickie, Susan, Rena, Pauline, Joan, Linda, Christine, Keith, Kelly, Ari, Debbie, Laureen, Penny, Susan, and Shirley, my favorite receptionist. Thanks for putting up with me, and thanks for all your work!

Curtis the dinosaur king and Chelsea, my goddaughter.

Helen Heller and Daphne Hart, for all their support. To my editor, Margaret Wolf, for her help, patience, and advice.

I must also thank the following: Mike Jokic for trusting me in my abilities as a tennis coach; I believe in you! To Matthew Baccarani, one of the most talented players I have had the chance to coach since he was nine years old. Matthew, the sky's the limit! Jennifer Baccarani, any U.S. school would be proud to have you as part of their team.

Special mention to: Evergreen Child Care Centers, the best in Toronto; Vic Braden for his kind words; Gigi Fernandez for her belief in my work with kids; Robert Massoud and Associates for their marketing advice. To Dan Santorum and Julie Jilly—U.S.P.T.R.; Gregg Presuto, a funny, warm, and kind person; Tim Heckler and Townsend Gilbert—U.S.P.T.A.; Kirk Anderson and Bill Leong—U.S.T.A.; Ann Pankhurst (and Roy)—London Tennis Association; Anne Marie Rouchon—French Tennis Federation; Patrick O'Rourke—New Zealand Tennis Association; Alan Trivett and Hatem McDadi—Tennis Canada; Liza Horan—*Tennis* magazine; Edvard Raastad—Norwegian Tennis Federation; and Ann Quinn—Tennis Australia. To Gator, for long ago showing a young hotshot coach the ropes; we've had some great talks, "uggie." And to Paul Mattina, Adrienne, Karl and Eddie (the best), Mel, Flo and Christine, Jim, Lori and Matthew Borsodi, Raf, Laura, Anthony, all my aunts and uncles around the world, Robert, Beth, Simone, Laurel, and all the students in my tennis academy.

Leading Edge Tennis, Inc.

Reggie Vasquez Jr. is available for consultation and presentations.

Contact: LEADING EDGE TENNIS, INC.
                Attention: Reggie Vasquez Jr.
Tel: (905) 883-6354
Fax: (905) 770-3754
E-mail: let@sympatico.ca
Website Leading Edge Tennis, Inc.:   www3.sympatico.ca/let
Mail: Suite 388
                1054 Centre Street
                Thornhill, Ontario, Canada, L4J 8E5

Leading Edge Tennis is a diverse organization that offers innovative tennis and physical conditioning products, coach and player
consultation, training workshops, and much more! Visit our website for free tennis articles and information. Ask for our catalogue.

3996956R00090

Printed in Great Britain
by Amazon.co.uk, Ltd.,
Marston Gate.